Praise for *Stand Out*

'Superbly written, wonderfully o[...]
is both intelligent and insightful:
standing out by being a better hu[...]

Trevor Newman, A.G. Barr drinks

'Packed with insightful and powerful ways to succeed and prosper
in a world where robots seem to be taking over. Don't be left behind,
this book is a must-read!'

**Kosta Christofi, Head of Leadership and Management
Development, Reed in Partnership**

'If you want clarity on the importance of human skills to achieve
both personal and business success in an age where technology
and digital seems to be the focus, then read this book for excellent
food for thought. Written by an author who knows what she's
talking about.'

**Joanne Williamson, Head of Standards &
Service, Stena Line Ltd**

'In an age where it is more important than ever to possess the skillset
needed to set yourself apart, this book has been written to help you
stand out. Do the exercises in the master class, learn and relearn the
most important human skills and the world will open up to you.'

**Mark C. Crowley, author of *Lead from The Heart:
Transformational Leadership For The 21st Century***

Praise for Stand Out

Stand Out

At Pearson, we have a simple mission: to help people make more of their lives through learning.

We combine innovative learning technology with trusted content and educational expertise to provide engaging and effective learning experiences that serve people wherever and whenever they are learning.

From classroom to boardroom, our curriculum materials, digital learning tools and testing programmes help to educate millions of people worldwide – more than any other private enterprise.

Every day our work helps learning flourish, and wherever learning flourishes, so do people.

To learn more, please visit us at **www.pearson.com/uk**

Stand Out

Five key skills to advance your career

Debra Stevens

Pearson

Harlow, England • London • New York • Boston • San Francisco • Toronto • Sydney
Dubai • Singapore • Hong Kong • Tokyo • Seoul • Taipei • New Delhi
Cape Town • São Paulo • Mexico City • Madrid • Amsterdam • Munich • Paris • Milan

PEARSON EDUCATION LIMITED
KAO Two
KAO Park
Harlow CM17 9NA
United Kingdom
Tel: +44 (0)1279 623623
Web: www.pearson.com/uk

First edition published 2021 (print and electronic)

© Pearson Education Limited 2021 (print and electronic)

The right of Debra Stevens to be identified as author of this work has been asserted by her in accordance with the Copyright, Designs and Patents Act 1988.

The print publication is protected by copyright. Prior to any prohibited reproduction, storage in a retrieval system, distribution or transmission in any form or by any means, electronic, mechanical, recording or otherwise, permission should be obtained from the publisher or, where applicable, a licence permitting restricted copying in the United Kingdom should be obtained from the Copyright Licensing Agency Ltd, Barnard's Inn, 86 Fetter Lane, London EC4A 1EN.

The ePublication is protected by copyright and must not be copied, reproduced, transferred, distributed, leased, licensed or publicly performed or used in any way except as specifically permitted in writing by the publishers, as allowed under the terms and conditions under which it was purchased, or as strictly permitted by applicable copyright law. Any unauthorised distribution or use of this text may be a direct infringement of the author's and the publisher's rights and those responsible may be liable in law accordingly.

All trademarks used herein are the property of their respective owners. The use of any trademark in this text does not vest in the author or publisher any trademark ownership rights in such trademarks, nor does the use of such trademarks imply any affiliation with or endorsement of this book by such owners.

Pearson Education is not responsible for the content of third-party internet sites.

ISBN: 978-1-292-31140-1 (print)
        978-1-292-31141-8 (PDF)
        978-1-292-31142-5 (ePub)

British Library Cataloguing-in-Publication Data
A catalogue record for the print edition is available from the British Library

Library of Congress Cataloging-in-Publication Data
A catalog record for the print edition is available from the Library of Congress
10 9 8 7 6 5 4 3
24 23 22 21

Cover design by Michelle Morgan, At the Pop Ltd.

Print edition typeset in 10/14 pt Charter ITC Pro by SPi Global
Printed by Ashford Colour Press Ltd, Gosport

NOTE THAT ANY PAGE CROSS REFERENCES REFER TO THE PRINT EDITION

For my two-year-old granddaughter Elsie:
Your smile is my inspiration

Contents

___

Contents

About the author

———

Debra Stevens, trainer, coach, inspiring speaker and founder of Dramatic Training Solutions, has been running award winning experiential workshops on conscious human skills for over 26 years. Her training and speaking have taken her all over the world. She has worked with thousands of people at all levels in companies such as Coca Cola, Network Rail, Santander, Stena Line and Hovis improving their human skills and helping them to be more successful leaders, salespeople, customer service operatives, businesses owners, parents, friends and partners.

Debra lives in Milton Keynes with her husband of 30 years, three grown up children, little granddaughter and two irrepressible Labradors, where having good human skills is essential to surviving as a family under the same roof.

Acknowledgements

Funny, I always read acknowledgements. I think it often speaks volumes about the author, so because I know I've got your attention let me acknowledge and thank you the reader first, then you can go and get a cup of tea. This is a dream come true for me, something I wrote in a future letter to myself ten years ago. I am inspired by people like you who are willing to go out of their comfort zone and work on themselves, so thank you for parting with your hard-earned cash to buy this book and most of all thank you for reading and acting on it.

My son Drew is the most creative person I know. A lot of his genius ideas are weaved throughout the masterclass, so Drew thank you for all the pep talks and reminding me I could do this. You are my son, my friend and my mentor all wrapped in one. Emily, you probably thought you didn't have a part to play but you did and I can't tell you how much I appreciate the words of support and for making the effort to read and report. Pete my husband, the backroom boy! Reading and checking, arranging the illustrations, sorting out transcripts, dealing with Debra the Diva and a shoulder to cry on – thank you, you're my rock.

Being told Pearson Education was going to publish my book made my year. I feel extremely honoured you chose me and I would not have wanted to be published by anyone else. I have written about collaboration in this book and working with Eloise Cook, my editor, has been a great example of a successful collaboration. Throughout the whole process I knew I was in the best hands, so thank you Eloise for your candid feedback and guidance. This is a much better book for it.

I was once told 'I want you to write a book' by a man who at the time I was totally in awe of and I was lucky later that he became my mentor and friend along with his amazing wife. Michael and Christine Heppell, without you this book would never have been written. Michael, thank you for not only taking the time to read the book and write the foreword, but also for going the extra brave mile and offering advice that made me think and inspired me to make important changes.

I also want to thank Jamie Cunningham, Kosta Christofi, Garry Goldman, Joanne Williamson and Peter Borg-Neal for agreeing to talk to me and giving such useful insight into the future of the workplace for the reader.

The amazing illustrations for the book were all hand-drawn by Charlie Lee (dreamsnart.wordpress.com)

Finally, to anyone who has ever been on one of my workshops, thank you for your energy, commitment and trust. I have learnt more from you than you could ever have learnt from me.

Publisher's acknowledgements

Text credits

1 Canongate Books: Haig, M. (2018). Notes on a nervous planet. Edinburgh: Canongate; **6, 23, 24, 35, 39 Pearson Education:** Bakhshi, H., Downing, J., Osborne, M. and Schneider, P. (2017).The Future of Skills: Employment in 2030. London: Pearson and Nesta; **9 Hunter S Thompson:** Quote by Hunter S Thompson; **19 Ali Binazi:** Quote by Dr Ali Binazi (author, happiness engineer & personal growth consultant); **27, 84, 90, 98, 142, 148, 170, 172 Peter Rice:** Drawn by Peter Rice; **28, 33, 38 World Economic Forum:** World Economic Forum: The future of jobs: Employment, Skills and Workforce Strategy for the Fourth Industrial Revolution, January 2016; **28 TED Conferences, LLC:** Alvin Toffler, (November 24, 2012) Theme: Unlearn The Familiar, TED Conferences, LLC; **28 Jamie Cunningham:** Quote by Jamie Cunningham; **29 Harvard Business Review:** Jacques Bughin Susan LundEric Hazan, (May 24, 2018). Automation Will Make Lifelong Learning a Necessary Part of Work, Harvard Business Review; **30 Joanne Williamson:** Quote by Joanne Williamson; **31 World Economic Forum:** The World Economic Forum report; **31, 101 Dale Carnegie:** Quote by Dale Carnegie; **32 Deloitte Touche Tohmatsu Limited:** The Deloitte Power Up UK Skills Report; **34 World Economic Forum:** World Economic Forum: The future of jobs; **35 Peter Borg Neal:** Quote by Peter Borg Neal; **36 Jacob Morgan:** Quoted by Jacob Morgan; **36, 37 Deloitte Touche Tohmatsu Limited:** The future of work in technology.

Publisher's acknowledgements

Retrieved from https://www2.deloitte.com/us/en/insights/focus/
technology-and-the-future-of-work/tech-leaders-reimagining-work-
workforce-workplace.html; **37 Kosta Christofi:** Quote by Kosta
Christofi; **40 TED Conferences, LLC:** Martin Ford: How we'll earn
money in a future without jobs, TED Conferences, LLC; **56 Michael
O'Leary:** Quote by Michael O'Leary; **68 Penguin Random House
LLC:** Carol S. Dweck, (December 26, 2007), Mindset: The New
Psychology of Success, Ballantine Books; **70 Mauro Van De Looij:**
Are top athletes born or made? - BelievePerform - The UK's leading
Sports Psychology Website. (2013, December 6). Retrieved from
https://believeperform.com/are-top-athletes-born-or-made/;
74 Garry Goldman: Quote by Garry Goldman; **78 Adam Kreek:**
4 Steps to Use Failure as Your Stepping Stone. (2019, January 29).
Retrieved from https://www.kreekspeak.com/4-steps-to-use-
failure-as-a-stepping-stone-2/; **84 Peter Rice: 93 Isabel Briggs
Myers:** Quote by Isabel Briggs Myers; **120 Alfred Brendel:** Quote
by Alfred Brendel; **128 Merriam Webster:** Merriam Webster;
139 Meryl Streep: Quote by Meryl Streep; **141 Mohsin Hami:** Quote
by Mohsin Hami; **141 Carl Rogers:** Quote by Carl Rogers; **141 Ian
Maclaren:** Quote by Ian Maclaren; **141 Stephen Covey:** Quote by
Stephen Covey; **160 TED Conferences, LLC:** Ha, T.-H. (2015,
December 26). What makes a great leader? A recommended reading
list. Retrieved from https://ideas.ted.com/what-makes-a-great-
leader-a-recommended-reading-list/; **160 Uber Technologies Inc.:**
Mission Statement from Uber Technologies Inc.; **160 Apple Inc.:**
Mission Statement from Apple Inc.; **174 CreateSpace Publishing
company:** Ian Berry. (2016). Influence: The Science behind
Persuasion: How to Make People Think What You Want. CreateSpace
Independent Publishing Platform.

Photo credits

191 The Human Works Academy: The Human Works Academy;
191 Carrie Wilkes: Carrie Wilkes; **192 Dramatic Training
Solutions:** Dramatic Training Solutions.

All other illustrations © Charlie Lee

Foreword

My father was a roofing contractor. He wanted me to join the family business, arguing it was 'a job for life'. He claimed that there was no way a robot could put a roof on a building. I could see his thinking. However, that was 30 years ago and I wonder how he'd consider things now.

There is no doubt that the robots are coming – and they will do many things bigger, better and certainly more efficiently than us humans. Almost every automated task and many mental tasks will be replaced. You can love it or loathe it, but you can't deny it. And for those who are prepared, during great times of change come greater opportunities.

Think of this book as the guide to maximise your prospects in life – not to fight the robots but rather to embrace the gloriousness of being human.

When Debra Stevens shared with me the idea of writing a book called *Stand Out*, I had more than a touch of author's envy. It's the idea you wish you'd thought of ... but I couldn't have written this book because of a simple truth. Debra has more experience in teaching people how to Stand Out by being human than anyone else I know. For over 20 years, she's travelled the world and worked with tens of thousands of people from every walk of life. Name a country, she's been there. List a sector, she's worked within it. And from CEOs to first week interns, she's trained, developed and helped them all to be better at work, home and life.

The masterclass element of *Stand Out* will give you an insight into the type of work Debra is renowned for. Be careful though not to treat it as a simple operating manual, lightly skimming over it, or (like a robot) reading each chapter to the end, without acting on any of it. That would be like a skydiver who does the course but never actually gets into the plane. It would be a costly mistake, as the secrets to becoming a better, more effective, employable, invaluable you are in these masterclass pages.

Be human and do more than just read it: scribble on the pages, be inquisitive, test the theories, do each exercise, apply every tool, get others involved, learn from failure and celebrate success.

If, like me, you're fascinated by what makes us human and how we can develop into a better person, then you are in for a treat. If there was ever a time to be less robot and more human, that time is now.

Michael Heppell
www.MichaelHeppell.com

part 1

We are not robots

Everything special about humans – our capacity for love and art and friendship and stories and all the rest – is not a product of modern life, it is a product of being human.

Matt Haig, author of *Notes on a Nervous Planet*

Robots will make work more human, not less; as they take on the boring mundane tasks you will be free to do what humans do best. This is why standing out by being a superhuman is more important than ever before so you can make the most of any opportunities that are coming your way and stay ahead of your competition – other humans! Skills such as empathy, listening, social connection and collaboration will sit at the top of skills required alongside science and technology. Are you ready?

chapter 1

We're only human

We just need a wake-up call

Pre corona virus and social distancing I am on the Jubilee Line in London heading to work, the carriage is packed, and people are standing desperate not to invade each other's personal space and avoiding eye contact. The only sound is the oscillating whoosh of the train, no one is talking to each other. This is the norm on the underground; it's part of our survival instinct to protect ourselves in these situations (even more so since the pandemic). The tube suddenly comes to a sharp stop and all the lights go out. It's pretty dark and then people start to turn on the torches from their phones, and there is a magical moment as the carriage lights up, but what's even more magical is people start to talk to each other.

It is as if a switch has been flicked as strangers start to connect, sparking the conversation around what is happening, to general chitchat once we are told it's an electrical fault and we will be on our way in five minutes. The lady I'm sat next to tells me she is on her way to meet her daughter who she is surprising with afternoon tea at the Ritz for her birthday. And a young man opposite me says how nervous he is for the job interview he's going to, having been out of work for six months after leaving university.

It was heart-warming to see people's empathy for each other kicking in once the ice was broken. It was just five minutes, but it was a fantastic reminder of how important connection is for us and how we just need the permission or the confidence to make it happen. After all, we are only human.

We sometimes need a catalyst to remind and encourage us to engage and empathise with others especially in our modern world, where we are bombarded with distractions from our technology and environment making it more difficult than ever before to be human. The cornona virus was a real wake up call and I remember in the first couple of weeks of lockdown it was like the world had woken up. Ironically the imposed isolation bought people together, neighbours talked for the first time and offered each other help, and communities arranged socially distanced street parties during the Jubilee. Technology like Zoom and WhatsApp kept people connected and we talked to more strangers than ever before.

The danger is that as things have gone back to normal, we have fallen back to sleep and with the added challenge of being even more reliant on technology. So I have written this book to be another catalyst, as I believe now is the time to celebrate and embrace humanness, warts and all, because it's those very warts that will help you to stand out and keep you competitive now and in the future. You're wonderful, emotional, imperfect and vulnerable and that's great.

The robots aren't coming – they are already here!

There is no denying automation: AI and robots aren't just coming, they are already here. Something moves in the semi-darkness of a closed shopping centre. As it comes to a clothing store it stops, flooding the window display in intense light. No alarm bells sound, no security guards rush forth. The Sunburst UV Bot, with its 1000 watts' worth of UVC light capable of 'tearing apart strands of virus DNA', comes here every night, as well as to a few other malls and hospitals in Singapore. It is doing something that human workers would have done before the covid19 pandemic: cleaning.

Before the corona virus the estimate in the UK was the predicted loss of 9 million jobs to AI and automation by 2030 and this is for both 'blue collar' and 'white collar' workers. This is now set to be accelerated as businesses look to protect themselves against future pandemics and let's face it robots don't get sick. Also, we are more accepting of automation now and some people even prefer it as it makes them feel safer to be served by a robot rather than a human.

Think robotic and data driven and it gives you a clue to the types of jobs and tasks that will be vulnerable, such as warehouse and factory jobs, drivers, agricultural jobs, lower-level manufacturing, checkout and check-in staff, call centre advisors, admin and sales support, order takers, recruitment admin and research assistants. And the list goes on. In the current environment with competition for jobs at its highest, for decades it might feel daunting, but at times like this I go back to the analogy of the bow needing to be pulled back to its most extreme tension before it can propel the arrow towards its target. We all need to be ready for that force for change and now is the time to get ready and stand out.

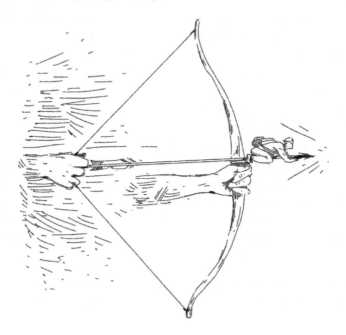

There will be new jobs created such as in store influencers, robot managers and management in general, media, healthcare, super salespeople. And there will be jobs we haven't even imagined yet.

Top tip

Go to the website https://futureskills.pearson.com/ It has a really great function where you can put in your current job and see if it's likely to shrink or grow, and it also tells you what skills you need now and the ones you'll need to develop.

The upside to this is that our unique human skills have become sought-after talents and are now being given the centre stage they deserve. These need to be super human skills if we are to stand out as we are all humans and in the current environment competition for opportunities will be tough. Automation will also create new jobs and make a lot of the work we currently do more enjoyable. For example, if robots take on the boring routine tasks, nurses and doctors will have more time to listen to patients' stories and address their concerns with understanding and empathy. Teachers can focus on the children, with more time to give extra support when needed. Lawyers can focus on their clients and salespeople can sell, rather than get bogged down with prospecting or using a CRM, and people in retail and hospitality will have time to engage with customers genuinely.

These are interesting times because there will be numerous opportunities and possibilities for everyone in the future including you. You don't have to go to university to learn human skills – you can do it every day on your way to work, in the coffee shop with your friends, at the supermarket, when having dinner with your family or Zooming with your customers – and it costs nothing except commitment and practice. If you start now you will be ahead of the curve.

Develop skills that are uniquely human. Although the advance and automation and artificial intelligence may feel

like a losing battle to some, individuals will need to focus on the uniquely human skills.

**The Future of Skills: Employment in 2030,
Pearson, Nesta and Oxford Martin School**

Use them or lose them

The quote above from The Future of Skills report backs up my point. Now is the time to develop your super human skills, like engaging, listening, empathising, collaborating and inspiring, all of which you will focus on in the masterclass in the second half of this book. The challenge for us all is that market research has found people spend more time on social media every day than they do on eating, drinking and socialising combined.

It's called social media but we're socialising less, talking less and connecting with people consciously less and it may be harder for us to take advantage of the new job opportunities. Do you find it hard to get anywhere on time without your SatNav or it's harder to remember your phone number? Maybe you can't read your own handwriting or do mental maths. These are all skills we used to have but they have been eroded because we don't use or need them anymore. The difference is we can't afford to lose our human skills.

Isn't it ironic that for the last 20 years we have been going through a technological revolution, with the focus on learning technical skills, IT, STEM (science, technology, engineering and maths), coding and so on and now we are being told if we want to survive automation, we need to shine at being human. Yet this same technology has given us smartphones and mobile devices leaving us with less time to practice the very skills we need now.

At the beginning of 2000 there was no YouTube, vlogging, Wikipedia, WhatsApp, Snapchat, Skype, Spotifi, Siri, Facebook, Twitter, Instagram, Netflix, broadband, 4G, SatNav, AirBnB or Uber. The list goes on and on. . .

All of the above are fantastic and magical, helping to make our lives richer and definitely easier. I still shudder at the memories of panic I felt missing meetings because I got stuck in traffic or couldn't find my way, trying to read a map and drive at the same time. The traffic app Waze has changed my life. We also have the opportunity to connect to loved ones all over the world. My daughter is working abroad on superyachts, meaning she is travelling ten months of the year and I miss her terribly. Without WhatsApp, Instagram and Facebook I would have no connection with her. Technology allows me to share the amazing places she is visiting, and even more importantly for her, she is able to keep up with the milestones in her niece's and my granddaughter's development She could even be at her second birthday party via WhatsApp.

Finally what would we have done without video conferencing platforms such as Zoom and Teams during the coronavirus demic? A lot of people's work communication depended on them and still does, but that doesn't mean we shouldn't use super human skills when using such technology; its just as important to stand out on a Zoom interview as it is face to face.

But we need to be careful because it's addictive. When you get a like on your latest photos on Facebook or Instagram, your brain creates dopamine, the hormone that controls pleasure and reward, and the brain always craves more. A friend of mine told me she became acutely aware of this addiction one night when her six-month-old baby daughter woke her up. She found herself sitting in the rocking chair phone in one hand, baby in the other, checking in to see who had liked the cute photos and videos she had put up earlier. She suddenly realised the opportunity to be conscious, present and in the moment with her little one was being sabotaged by social media. Its more important than ever to be aware of our addiction, as post corona virus the research showed that during lockdown our use of social media was up by a staggering 20%.

We've only got ourselves to blame

Despite all of this we just can't blame technology for the eroding of our human skills – we only have ourselves to blame. The hard facts are that company heads text or email during corporate board meetings, (face to face and even more on video conferencing) employees shop online during office hours or in the middle of presentations, students go on Facebook amid class hours, and parents text, talk on their mobile devices or email at mealtimes. And children complain about not having their parents' full attention. But at the same time, too, these same children deny each other their full attention.

All skills – technical, practical or soft – will be affected by not using them. This is why over half of this book is an experiential masterclass exercising your human skills so they can improve. We need to be actively practising our social skills if we want them to be natural and easy. Think of what happens when you get on a train or a bus. Do you look, smile and acknowledge the person near to you, or go straight to your phone and check social media instead? I know I do the latter and I bet you do too. Since the pandemic it is even more tempting to hide just like we did behind the masks. As humans we need to find a way to navigate the advantages of technology and the effect it can have on us if we rely on it too much as the way to connect and communicate.

The rise of the human robot

The Killers released a song over 10 years ago with a controversial lyric questioning our humanness in the face of conforming to rules and processes in our lives. This song's title was inspired by a quote from American Journalist Hunter S Thompson who said, 'America is raising a generation of dancers afraid to take one step out of line', which is a really interesting idea. I believe we're all in danger of becoming like this. Technology and the very structure and processes

we've put in place to make us better managers, leaders, customer service advisors and salespeople or business owners are turning us into human robots.

There is no judgment in that we can all be guilty of it sometimes including me. Often it is the pressure we are under to be quick and efficient. Have you noticed that at most airports there are very few humans present as they have become so automated? If, like me you're not an expert at printing baggage labels and attaching them to your case, you're bound to need help. First, you need to find someone, and when you do are they smiling, giving you eye contact and being supportive and empathetic? Probably not if it's anything like my experience (and I travel a lot). They will hardly acknowledge you, robotically dealing with your issue and moving on, almost as if they're sleepwalking, going through the motions, and you end up with a cold, detached human, and no connection.

Or you walk into a retail outlet to be greeted in a singsong almost automated way, dishing out the same old greeting they use on everyone and we all know it's because they've been told what to say and how to say it. Sadly, I'd prefer a real robot any day than either of these. Wouldn't you?

On top of all of this during the corona virus panemic we experienced a very mixed bag. At some retailers and service providers we were treated like potential criminals and the interaction was rude and aggressive and in others it was the opposite, warm, authentic and full of understanding. I don't know about you but I know which brands I am now more loyal to.

Don't leave your humanness at the door

For some reason over the years we have been led to believe that at work we must diminish our humanity, behaving (and appearing) like robots prized for their automation and conformity. When we are in a work space (home or office), we leave our real and authentic selves at the metaphorical door, ramp up our 'professional' mindset and keep our human traits gagged until we leave or switch off for the evening. This isn't just face to face it's the same when working from home and using video conferencing. One of my most popular courses is in helping people to be more real and human when in a video meeting. The belief that we need to be as efficient as an LED bulb, as knowledgeable as Wikipedia, as productive as an assembly line, and as human as a doorknob might have worked in the industrial age, but today, we can't afford to forget the one ingredient that's essential for business success – humanness.

So, could we be on our way to becoming human robots? You are a human robot when you're not present, when you're going through the motions, putting efficiency before connection, or you are flicking from one social media app to the next and then back to the first one again to see if anyone else has commented on your video in the last 60 seconds. It's also when you're not listening and you're in your head thinking about what you're going to say or avoiding eye contact. It's not only customer service people who act this way. A lovely lady working on the checkout at Morrison's supermarket me how soul-destroying it was for her when so many customers are on their phones when checking their shopping through and don't even look at her. How much more important was eye contact when wearing a mask and yet it felt even more difficult to give.

You might be familiar with the Turing test (developed by Alan Turing in 1950) as an important way to test artificial intelligence against humans, to understand how well robots are able to mimic our behaviour. But some experts are putting forward the case that we need another type of test that tells us to what extent we are becoming like machines. Our processes and the need to make things efficient and cheap are taking away what we crave: real human connection. That's not just because the robots are more like humans – it's because we are more like them.

We need to raise our awareness and take action to relearn our human skills now before we get left behind. This book is a practical way to do this, giving you control of your future, enabling you to be happier and find and do the work you love.

How to get the most from this book

The most likely scenario for the future is humans working alongside robots and automation. Based on the research I've done and my experience, listed below are the five key 'human only' skills (AI and robots can't do them) that you need to develop right now. These skills are transferable from job to job as the working landscape changes rapidly. They will complement automation as it takes on the repetitive tasks, giving you the time and space to maximise these skills. They are in high demand and short supply, so if you want to get ahead and stay ahead you need to:

- Engage: Your social skills and the ability to connect authentically
- Listen: Slowing down and asking questions from a place of curiosity
- Empathise: A genuine desire to understand someone else's experience

- Collaborate: Build, manage and collaborate in the teams of the future
- Inspire: Storytelling, influencing, persuading and articulating your ideas

The above are the foundation stones you will develop as you work through the book. But I don't want this to be just another self-help book that you buy because the title and the cover speak to you and after just a few chapters it ends up in a bedroom drawer or on the shelf of a charity shop. I want this book to really make a difference to your life. This means this is more than just a read – it's an experiential journey. That is why more than half this book is a human master-class and you will need to participate actively, use it as the catalyst to develop your confidence and bravery in these five future-proof human skills.

The opportunities

There is a lot of doom and gloom in some of the headlines – fear sells newspapers and gets blogs read. But there are exciting opportunities coming for those that are ready, so the research I have done is based on how you can make the most of what is coming. There is a scent of opportunity in the air and you will be in the know and ahead of the game so you can develop the five super human skills that keep you afloat and make you stand out.

The human robot quiz

This is a fun way to do some self-reflection and have some aware-ness on where you might be developing some human robot behaviours. If we try to compete with robots by being robots, we have no chance. We need to embrace what makes us human.

A roadmap to humanness

This is a unique opportunity to really focus on yourself, decide what sort of employee and human you want to be and be known for. It will help you to make sense of the quiz and how you can use the results to improve your human skills, but it will also do the following:

- Introduce you to the idea of having a growth mindset, taking responsibility for your own learning, which is absolutely essential in the future working environment.
- Encourage you to get feedback and see it as an opportunity to grow.
- Help you identify the unique strengths you already have and how you can maximise them.
- Start the process of creating your elevator pitch and personal story, which you can use in your LinkedIn profile, CV, interviews or even when introducing yourself.

The human masterclass

As I keep saying, the power of this book is not in the understanding – it's in the doing. You can't get fit by reading about the gym – you've got to work out. Being consciously human is the same – it's an activity and it takes effort, courage and commitment. Also, if you stop going to the gym for any length of time you quickly lose the fitness and it's hard to get back into it again. This means (and I hate to say it) it's a life's work to ensure you're as fit as can be and being consciously human is no different.

In the masterclass I use the gym as an analogy and the exercises run over a five-week period, one week for each of the skills with five exercises each day to help you to break old habits and create new ones in their place. There are even exercises to use on technology where face to face isn't possible or appropriate. It's really important to do the whole programme, but once it's completed you can retake the human robot quiz whenever you feel you're slipping and go back to the areas you need the most, or if your circumstances change and you need a specific skill. This is a book for life, not just for Christmas.

I have interviewed some brilliant people, who, because of their jobs and experience, are in a great position to give you advice. They've shared with me the skills they believe are most important, both now and in the future. You'll find their experience and advice throughout the book. I may be an expert on how to develop human skills, but just like you I'm always learning when it comes to technology and the future of work.

The research

Researching the current and future working environment for this book has been fascinating, confusing and sometimes terrifying. So it's important that I present you the information in an interesting, approachable and positive way, showing what's happening now and likely to happen over the next few years, so you can get on with what's important straightaway – developing your human skills in the masterclass.

There are two critical reports that I'll be referring to: The Future of Skills: Employment in 2030, Pearson, Nesta and Oxford Martin School, and The Future of Jobs Report by The World Economic Forum. Post pandemic these reports are more important than ever as the evidence is that automation is being accelerated. Companies large and small are expanding how they use robots to increase social distancing and reduce the number of staff who have to physically come to work. Robots are being used to perform roles workers cannot do at home.

If you want to, you can read the complete reports, but I've done the hard work, so you get the information needed to understand enough about the future environment, and most importantly, why you'll need to take control of your own learning and development and survive and thrive in the fourth industrial revolution. Not since the second world war has it been more important to become self-motivated and willing to take responsibility for your own leanring, if you don't you will get left behind!

Go buy a journal

So now's the time to go out and buy yourselves a really nice journal (I love a journal, I really should have shares in Paperchase), and this journal is going to be your best friend throughout the rest of this book and beyond. You should use it to take notes, reflect on and keep track of your journey, be a record to look back on, a reminder of where you want to be and the areas which you still need to focus on.

You might automatically assume a digital journal will be easier, but a physical one makes this more tangible, and there's something really lovely and gratifying about holding and writing in a beautiful book. Also, real writing stimulates and engages the brain in a different way, making it easier to remember information. Another advantage is that it slows you down, and in our fast-paced world it may seem counter-intuitive but slowing down is good. It actually increases activity in the brain's motor cortex, an effect that's similar to meditation. If you do opt for a digital version, be careful, don't be tempted to go on social media, check your emails, or play a game when you should be filling it out.

Why me?

It feels like a big deal sitting here making a start on this book. My English teacher Mr Lloyd, a small round man with jet-black hair and a booming voice, said to me; 'Debra, whatever you do, don't do anything that involves writing. Make sure you speak for a living instead, because your writing is terrible and you never shut up!' If only he could see me now (sadly, he passed away). Funny though, he was right as I now make my living by training and facilitating.

I've learnt over the years that telling someone how to do something doesn't work. We need to learn through doing and my workshops reflect this because they are experiential, meaning participants learn through interactive exercises and reflecting on what they've learnt.

I hope you'll agree this is a very human book. I am still learning and I know I will never be perfect and I don't want to be. It's a real privilege to work in my business with people on skills that will not only help them at work but also help them to be better sons, daughters, parents and friends. This book reflects how I run my workshops and the masterclass is made up of what I call 'bankers'.

In other words, exercises that really work, they are not easy, but my aim is to challenge you, sometimes taking you outside your comfort zone.

Read, and more importantly act, and you'll be a better human and a more employable one. This is a book for everyone. Even if you have incredible technological skills, being a more conscious human will make you stand out and stick in the most rewarding jobs with the most progressive companies. If you're in a job that's under threat you can reinvent yourself, but don't expect your current employers or potential new employers to train you – they'll expect you to be a self-directed learner working on yourself.

The best compliment for me would be to see my book well-worn, full of notes and tabs, maybe even a few loose pages, being kept in a favourite bag along with a laptop, phone and notebook.

You really are a human miracle!

I am so in awe of the technological advancement and how if we look on the bright side it will make our lives easier, happier, wealthier and richer, but let's not forget how special we are as humans. Dr Ali Binazi, author, happiness engineer and personal growth consultant, makes this point in a fantastic blog post (look him up, he's brilliant).

He says the chances of you being born are around one in 700 trillion, and as that's hard to imagine he uses the following analogy.

Imagine there was one life preserver thrown somewhere in some ocean and there is exactly one turtle in all of these oceans, swimming underwater somewhere. The probability that you came about and exist today is the same as that turtle sticking its head out of the water — in the middle of that life preserver. On one try.

Ali Binazi

Amazing? The chance of this happening is so unlikely it is almost impossible. The definition of a miracle is an event that is deemed to be impossible, so there you go, you are a human miracle. Let's embrace those human skills. You are unique and I am excited to invite you on this journey to humanness, so let's get started.

chapter 2

—

The future of work

This is a time of opportunity

Despite what you read in the newspapers and online, the world is not going to end and if you have the right skills and attitude the future is full of opportunities. This book will help you discover the five key human skills to not just survive but thrive in this 'fourth industrial revolution'.

For years, in science fiction films such as *Terminator, Star Wars, Artificial Intelligence, Blade Runner,* and more recently the TV series *Humans,* we've been asking the same question, will robots take over the planet from humans and will we end up on the scrapheap? Some recent headlines are pretty scary too.

Robots will destroy our jobs – and we're not ready for it!

Bank Chief: Robots to steal 15m of your jobs!
Doom-laden Carrey warns middle classes will be hollowed out by new technology

Death by robot: the new mechanised danger in our changing world

As the use of autonomous machines increases in society, so too has the chance of robot-related fatalities.

Stephen Hawking warned us that the rise of robots may be disastrous for mankind.

It's no wonder we're now having thoughts such as 'The robots are coming! We're all going to lose our jobs! They're going to take over the world! We need to get rid of them now before they turn on us! It's the end of mankind as we know it!'

Of course, the headlines are dramatic, feeding the fear, because they sell newspapers. But things are definitely changing. I was in a well-known sports retailer recently and since the corona virus they have introduced a self-service check out. Nothing unusual in that you might think but this was for sports clothes; you throw in the garments one by one, it shows you the items on a screen and you then pay, so simple and not a human in sight!

Robots can do these jobs and to some its efficienct, quick, and safe, but there will also be opportunities for people with great human skills to help us when things go wrong or we have a question or want help finding things. I find it sad to see the customer service people in these shops standing and chatting while customers who obviously have questions or information are being ignored, the very thing that will replace them is are doing the easy bit, so how about some eye contact, enthusiasm and warmth? This is what will make you stand out. The point is we will have the choice – a sign of the times.

Research nugget

We predict around one-tenth of the workforce are in occupations that are likely to grow as a percentage of the workforce. Around one-fifth are in occupations that will likely shrink. This means that roughly seven in ten people are currently in jobs where we simply cannot know for certain what will happen.

The Future of Skills: Employment in 2030, Pearson, Nesta and Oxford Martin School

Are we the horses of the future?

A brilliant TED talk by Martin Ford, a leading expert on the robot revolution and its impact on society, called 'How we'll earn money in the future without jobs?' He talks about how we've had revolutions before – the industrial revolution and the technology revolution – and there was a lot of scaremongering about the loss of jobs and the impact on society. We no longer weave fabrics by hand or even with looms as it's now done by automated machines. The land used to be tilled by hand and then with horses and now it's sometimes even done by self-driving tractors. As humans, we have been able to adapt and the jobs are now better and more meaningful.

Martin goes on to say that after the industrial revolution one part of the workforce never recovered and is no longer meaningful in the world of employment and it's the horse. Before the industrial revolution horses were involved in most industries and are now pretty much redundant (sorry to all you equestrians out there). So, it begs the question, could we be the horses of the future? Horses aren't as intelligent as humans, or as adaptable, but what has changed is this time the competition isn't just machines – it's machines that can think and more importantly learn.

If you think routine, repetitive and predictable jobs are at risk, you'd be right and they account for nearly 50% of all current jobs. However, you'd also be wrong. Why? Because the lines are shifting and machines are now learning. Old automation and robotics are large and chunky – they build cars and milk cows – but the new automation, being more refined, is equivalent to white collar workers rather than blue collar. They're mostly algorithms and commonly known as Artificial Intelligence (AI), invisible, ethereal, and able to cross borders, via the internet and apps. It's this type of robot that's likely to be involved in data analysis and ultimately will affect jobs in customer service, healthcare, sales and transportation.

Research nugget

Nearly 71% of work is currently carried out by humans and 29% by machines. By 2022 this is set to change to 58% by humans and 42% by machines. It's incredible to think that this can happen in just two short years.

The Future of Skills: Employment in 2030, Pearson, Nesta and Oxford Martin School

---

Take a look at the table below. They may have snuck up on you or you didn't realise that they were robots, but they have been with us for a while and there are more coming all the time.

Now	Future	At risk of change
The touchscreen ordering system at McDonalds	Robot waiters (already being trialled in Yamm World Buffet in Dundee)	Restaurant servers and coffee barristers
Automated checkouts at the supermarket	Shelf-stacking robots	Retail shop assistants and shelf-stackers
Amazon warehouse robots	Amazon Scout uses self-driving technology to navigate through neighbourhoods to deliver packages	Warehouse workers Delivery drivers
Siri, Alexa, Google Assistant	Sofia, a humanoid-like robot that's capable of holding a conversation	Home helps, health workers, PAs, office assistants, sales administrators
Chatbots, helping with customer service; reminders of what to buy or suggestions to buy when online shopping; Netflix recommending programmes to watch	Virtual assistant software	Customer service advisors, call centre staff
Automated hiring tools to screen applicants	A 16-inch tall robot-recruiter named Tengai	Recruitment administration, recruiters
Semi-automated mason (SAM)	The Hadrian X can lay a thousand standard bricks in one hour, a task that would take two bricklayers a least a whole day	Construction workers, brick layers

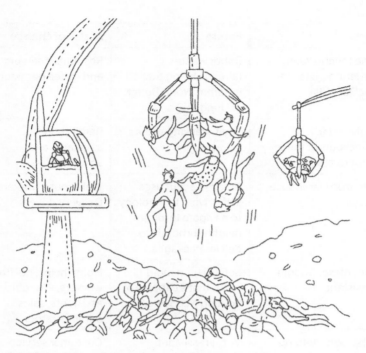

Robots will complement you, not replace you

We are a long way from being on the human scrapheap and research indicates that the future is full of possibilities. There is a very big difference between robots taking our jobs and doing tasks within our jobs, those we don't do well and hate anyway.

For example, if you work in sales you probably spend a lot of your time prospecting for and qualifying leads, sending out follow-up emails and proposals or updating your CRM. If you had an AI assistant to do all of this for you, what would be left for you to do? It would be the emotional and creative stuff. You could spend more of your time building customer relationships, understanding their problems, coming up with inspiring and creative solutions. If AI does the mundane tasks you have to do grudgingly, you can focus on the core of your job, which only a human can do.

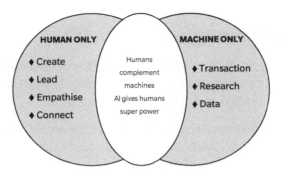

HUMAN ONLY
♦ Create
♦ Lead
♦ Empathise
♦ Connect

Humans complement machines
AI gives humans super power

MACHINE ONLY
♦ Transaction
♦ Research
♦ Data

Humans versus machines

Retail and hospitality account for nearly 20% of jobs in the UK and because of automated checkouts, online shopping and high street shop closures, the traditional jobs are at risk. The RSA have been collaborating with major retailers such as Tesco, John Lewis, River Island and Ted Baker to try to forecast the future of working in retail. An 'in-store influencer' was one of the new opportunities presented for workers in high street stores and another was 'line manager for robots'. The influencer's role was described as building a brand's relationship with customers directly, rather than lower-skilled work such as stock control or checkouts. In supermarkets this might require shop-floor workers to gain skills in cooking and nutrition so that they can host cooking classes or advise customers about diets and recipes using new ingredients.

(Info on other new jobs coming from Pearson 2030 report)

The new jobs sound really exciting and motivating and there are examples like this right across all the areas of work: manufacturing, technology, healthcare and hospitality. If you have a child in primary school, when they start work it will be in a job that probably doesn't yet exist. The world of work is changing, but this will deliver new opportunities and give you more time to focus on higher-value work that requires empathy, emotion, collaboration and creativity, the very qualities that make us human. This means a future we can all look forward to.

Research nugget

On average, by 2020, more than a third of the desired core skillsets of most occupations will be comprised of skills that are not yet considered crucial to a job today.

The Future of Jobs Report, The World Economic Forum

Learn, unlearn and relearn – the five survival skills of the future

The illiterate of the 21st century are not those who can't read and write, but those who cannot learn, unlearn and relearn.

Alvin Toffler, writer and futurist

Be honest, up to this point, what skills do you think were most important for students to master for the twenty-first century? The chances are you thought the STEM subjects (science, technology, engineering and maths), add a bit of code into the mix and you're sorted jobwise. Well, you're not wrong, but it's not the full picture either. As STEM becomes less important for most of us, it gives us the opportunity to focus on our human skills, and the good news is they can be mastered with commitment and practice. This is where the masterclass comes in later in this book.

I had a really interesting interview with Jamie Cunningham, former head of employment brand for Tesco. He now runs his own consultancy advising large companies on how to retain and attract the best people for their business. Jamie told me that for people to be successful in the future they would need to focus on change management and soft skills like communication.

He says, 'What makes us human is our need to innovate. We need to make our employee experience focused on developing our own human software, which is communication skills, to enable the innovation that is possible from our technical hardware skills.'

I love this quote from Jamie and if we need to work on upgrading our software the five key skills we're going to work on in the masterclass (Engage, Listen, Empathise, Collaborate, Inspire) are a great start as they are in demand now and will be even more in the future and are referenced frequently in the most respected reports. Of course, they're all linked and you can't really engage without listening, or inspire without engaging, or even empathise without listening.

Research nugget

These are often seen as 'soft' skills that schools and education systems in general are not set up to impart. Yet in a more auto-mated future, when machines are capable of taking on many more rote tasks, these skills will become increasingly important – precisely because machines are still far from able to provide expertise and coaching, or manage complex relationships.

Harvard Business Review

Engage – your social skills and the ability to connect authentically

We're all different and not all of us find it easy or natural to talk to strangers and people we don't know that well. The future of work will involve more teamwork, not less and as teams change more often, it's essential you find a way to authentically connect with others. Uncomfortable as it may be to some, small talk and chitchat are ritualistic ways to start and build relationships. This is something we used to do naturally, but now for many of us it's less likely for the following reasons:

- The car has replaced the bus.
- Twitter is the new water cooler.
- Working at home is becoming the norm as opposed to the office or factory.

- Zoom is replacing face-to-face meetings and training.
- TV has replaced theatre.
- Netflix has replaced cinema.
- We're more likely to meet on social media than down the pub.
- Tinder or Plenty of Fish have replaced flirting in bars and clubs.

Modern life often means fewer opportunities to connect, meaning we have to work that bit harder at it, often pushing us outside our comfort zone. If you work or aspire to work in retail or hospitality, engaging with strangers has always been important, but in future it will be something that'll make you stand out. In the earlier table you may have noticed that automation is already having an impact and it will become increasingly common in restaurants and retail. But they will still need humans to work alongside technology because customers still want the human touch. Employers will be looking for people with exceptional social skills, those able to deliver high levels of personal service.

I have worked very closely with Joanne Williamson, customer experience manager for Stena Line, for over 12 years helping with its customer service training. The company puts the customer at the heart of its business and I interviewed Jo to give you more insight into what skills a large travel and hospitality company wants from its employees now and in the future. Jo told me that despite challenges in the travel industry Stena have ambitious plans for expansion with new ships coming and these will use a combination of automation and great people to give the customers a quick, efficient and very human service.

She says, 'I think the way in which we are looking at it, it is not about replacing people with technology, but more importantly supporting technology within the customer experience journey with the best quality human interactions at the touch points where it can make the most impact and adds the most value to our customers.'

She also told me that it was increasingly difficult to find young people with the skills they need, 'I think what it's probably highlighted for us, which is not new, is that the areas of communication, taking initiative and having confidence in engaging with customers is often lacking. With all the devices we have, it's affecting the way we connect with each other and our social skills, specifically I notice it with the younger generation.'

Research nugget

Roles which leverage distinctly human skills, such as customer service workers, sales and marketing professionals, training and development managers, people and culture and organisational development specialists, will be in great demand.

We also predict a need for high-level customer advisors who have skills in gathering information, listening to customers, interpreting their needs and providing advice.

The Future of Jobs Report, The World Economic Forum

Listen – slowing down and asking questions from a place of curiosity, listening to understand rather than to respond

Conscious listening cannot be underestimated and will play an important role helping you to get ahead in your career. It's another skill which can be acquired and developed with patience and practice, and it links to all other human skills. For example, one of the best ways to connect and engage is to listen actively and is especially useful to introverts. Listening can help inspire others and sell your ideas and is essential for empathy and collaboration. Being a good active listener will make you stand out from the crowd, drawing people to you like nothing else, as Dale Carnegie said, 'To be interesting be interested.'

I remember a few years ago I was working for a large media company and in the workshops I was running I kept hearing stories about the amazing corporate finance officer (CFO) and what a fantastic and inspiring person he was. I must have heard similar things in over 30 workshops. CFOs are not normally known for being charismatic, but this guy seemed to have something special. I have to say I was curious and really wanted to meet him.

I got my chance at a gala dinner following a large conference as I was lucky enough to be sat next to him. After being with him for just ten minutes I understood why everyone loved him so much: he was a fantastic listener. He was curious and genuinely interested in everything I had to say, he asked me questions about my ideas and passions and before we had got to the main course he made me feel like the most interesting person in the world. That night I saw people drawn to him like moths to a flame. He was irresistible. What a gift!

Research nugget

Boosting transferable skills report puts active listening skills at number 3 in the top 40 most important transferable skills for the future.

Power Up: UK Skills, Deloitte

Listening is important because it forms the foundation of good relationships. Why? Because it shows you care. Empathy and listening go hand in hand. You can't display empathy or emotional intelligence if you do not listen. The quality of our listening determines the quality of your influence. Listening transmits that kind of respect and builds trust. This means it's an essential, transferable skill, which is already highly sought after by recruiters and employers. It will take a lot of conscious effort but it's worth it.

Due to information overload and our shortened attention spans, most of us (myself included) are guilty of starting a conversation, asking a question or putting a thought forward and then not listening to the answer. Why? Because we want to talk, we are too busy thinking about our reply and assuming we know what is coming.

Research nugget

Content skills (which include ICT, literacy and active learning), cognitive abilities (such as creativity and mathematical reasoning) and process skills (such as active listening and critical thinking) will be a growing part of the core skills requirements for many industries.

The Future of Jobs Report, The World Economic Forum

Empathise – a genuine desire to understand someone else's experience

There's not an article about the future of work which doesn't mention how massively important empathy is. It is finally experiencing a well-deserved moment on the centre stage of work skills. Our work is better when we understand who we're making it for, and empathy helps us do just this. We work better together when we're open to many perspectives and experiences outside our own. Customer service, sales, healthworkers, lawyers and leaders all need to have empathy. We saw during the corona virus how leaders who put the well-being of their people before profit created more loyal and hardworking teams and brands that showed empathy towards their customers and had more customer loyalty later on.

I heard a story of a really good example of this – a woman was at work when she got a call from her mother, and she immediately felt her stomach turn as her mum never phoned her at work. She asked her what was wrong, and her mum told her "they found a tumor in my brain". Her mind struggled to grasp what she heard and then she lost it and walked out of the meeting with her car keys, running towards the exit. Her boss happened to walk past her, and she told him with tears in her eyes that she had to go as it was an emergency. He looked at her for one second and said 'Got it. Take all the time you need. We'll handle things here.' No questions asked. No explanations needed; it was one of the worst days of her life and he made it easier.

As employees we don't remember the perks like free lunches, parties and free massages, what we remember is the empathy, compassion and kindness. This was never truer than during the corona virus; this is the age of leading from the heart.

Some of the most successful, future-oriented thinkers and business people believe that to be successful in the new world of work takes a distinctly human touch. Even as automation changes the future of work and the roles people play in the workplace, there are job skills that machines can't imitate. To stand out from the competition – both robotic and human – workers in the future will need to practice and polish empathy, to better relate to one another. We're lucky: the number one job skill of the future is one that we as humans are uniquely suited to master.

Research nugget

Emotional intelligence will be an important skill of the future. A person's ability to be aware of, control and express their own emotions, as well as being cognisant of the emotions of others, describes their emotional intelligence. You exhibit high emotional intelligence if you have empathy, integrity and work well with others. A machine can't easily replace a human's ability to connect with another human being, so those who have high EQs will be in demand.

The Future of Jobs Report, The World Economic Forum

The human touch

I was lucky to be able to speak to Peter Borg Neal, founder and CEO of Oakman Inns, who has created a chain of over 23 high-quality food-serving pubs and is an inspiring entrepreneur. He told me he thinks technology would play an important part in his business moving forward, specifically for making things easier for his customers when ordering or paying, and also when managing music and lighting to make the most of the environment. He was also keen to tell me why the customer experience needed to be human.

'I still think it's the smaller things that matter when you're there. I think people want to talk and interact with the waiter or waitress or somebody behind the bar. I think it's still a really important part of the experience.'

When I asked him what skills he valued most in his people he told me he looks for people who care, 'I think that they are people who can have empathy, those who are sensitive to the needs of others. We are looking for people who naturally enjoy being hospitable, those who take pleasure in seeing others enjoying themselves. It's a human thing; it's a kind thing.'

By 2030, there will be at least 300 million more people aged 65 years and older than in 2014. This will create significant new demand for a range of occupations, including doctors, nurses and health technicians, but also home health aides, personal care aides and nursing assistants.

Robots will be able to do a lot of the mundane and manual work. For example, Robear is a nursing care robot, developed by RIKEN-SRK of Japan. The idea behind the robot is to help people, particularly the elderly, regain some independence. It is said to be strong enough to lift patients out of bed and gentle enough to put them down carefully, but it doesn't understand empathy. Imagine a job where you're paid, not for the manual mundane caring, but to listen, have conversations and empathetically seek to understand.

Research nugget

In the future, robots will be able to diagnose disease, build bridges, etc, but they won't have the unique human skills to engineer the bridge or care for sick children.

The Future of Skills: Employment in 2030, Pearson, Nesta and Oxford Martin School

Collaborate – build, manage and communicate in the teams of the future

> It sounds trite, but the one thing machines will have a tough time doing is building relationships, developing emotional intelligence – empathy, embracing vulnerability, building strong connections with your co-workers and your network –will go a long way to keeping you highly marketable
>
> Jacob Morgan, author of *The Future of Work*

You've probably heard the saying 'There's no I in team', and here's a new one for you: There's no AI in team. Teamwork and collaboration encourage creativity and innovation, leading to more engaged (and happier) employees. Teamwork is a skill we shouldn't neglect in the era of artificial intelligence, because it plays a major part in what sets us apart from robots, making us irreplaceable in the workplace.

Major problems are (almost) never solved independently. It takes a team of people, representing different points of view, to get to an answer. Learning to collaborate and coordinate, in order to deliver results, is critical in many industries, making it the backbone of business school education. As we see in the cutting-edge research being conducted, machines and AI are becoming more integral to work teams, making them more productive. Machines will be our team members and the better humans know how to build, manage and work in teams, the more they'll be able to make the most of human/machine partnerships.

Research nugget

Historically, technology teams took pride in developing and delivering IT capabilities to serve business needs as specialist technologists. In the future they'll become collaborative cocreators, adding value to the business and this will mean different, more human skills like collaboration.

The Future of Work in Technology, Deloitte Insights (Khalid Kark, Bill Briggs, Atilla Terzioglu, Minu Puranik)

The importance of relationships

I wanted to talk to Kosta Christofi at Reed In Partnership, part of the Reed Group of companies, because he is right at the cutting edge of training and development and knows what people will need to secure their future. He told me how Reed in Partnership supports individuals and their families to prosper, often under challenging circumstances. It helps people to get work, improve their health, develop skills and fulfill their potential.

Kosta believes despite automation coming, relationships will still be important to teams and business as a whole, 'Anything that involves a defined process is at a high risk of being overtaken. I personally think we're a long way off yet from replacing the human touch. Ultimately, I see roles where you're building actual relationships between people still being in high demand. For us more than anything it is people's personal skills that are the most important – empathy and understanding coupled with a strong commitment to help improve people's lives.'

Research nugget

In the past, soft skills that support collaboration and communication typically took a back seat to specialised technical skills. Today, soft skills are having a breakout moment. These enduring, essentially human skills are increasing in value in part because they cannot be replicated by machines.

The Future of Work in Technology, Deloitte Insights (Khalid Kark, Bill Briggs, Atilla Terzioglu, Minu Puranik)

Inspire – storytelling, influencing, persuading and articulating your ideas

The best-selling non-fiction paperback series ever sold over 500 million copies globally. What do you think it is? The answer is *Chicken Soup for the Soul*. The book is basically a collection of inspirational stories.

TED talks famously feature powerful stories and we just can't get enough of them. Stories launch brands, charities and causes; they literally make the world go round.

The workplace in the future will rely more on effective communication than ever before and with all of the information, products, ideas that are out there today it will be vital to know how to capture the attention of others. Robots may be able to learn everything from all the best books on influencing, by the likes of Robert Cialdini and Dale Carnegie who are masters of inspiration, but they still can't compete with our natural talent for storytelling.

Storytelling is the ability to use narratives, to deliver our personal experiences or the stories of others with emotion and with passion in a way which resonates with an audience. Wrapping data with emotion leads to better recollection, empathy and connection. Humans have told stories to educate, motivate and persuade for as long as we have been called human.

Research nugget

Overall, social skills – such as persuasion, emotional intelligence and teaching others – will be in higher demand across industries than narrow technical skills, such as programming or equipment operation and control.

The Future of Jobs Report, The World Economic Forum

Being able to inspire others can help you connect with colleagues at work and helps you to be respected and listened to. You're able to talk about your accomplishments, goals and ideas in a way that influences those around you to be excited and passionate as well. It's not just salespeople who need to be persuasive – we all do. Even if you just think about a job interview, the ability to influence and persuade as well as tell stories about your skills and talents is more likely to land you a job than a well-written CV.

The online recruitment agency Glassdoor says that storytelling is the secret to wowing a hiring manager. So if nothing else, we need to craft our own personal 'this is who I am and why you should employ me story'.

Research nugget

*Customer service and sales occupations, for example. According to O*NET data, customer and personal service, oral comprehension and oral expression are the three most important features for this group. Our model predicts that increasing judgment and decision-making, fluency of ideas and originality in the presence of these features will have the greatest positive impact on future demand.*

The Future of Skills: Employment in 2030, Pearson, Nesta and Oxford Martin School

Have I convinced you? Because now's the time to get ahead of the competition and put yourself in the best place to maximise the opportunities that are coming. But this is not all about the future as the skills mentioned earlier have always been important and will make a huge difference now and not just in your career, but in your life. The next step is to take the human robot survey and start to build your roadmap to humanness and a bright exciting future.

Recommended reading and viewing

Reports

- The Future of Skills: Employment in 2030, Pearson, Nesta and Oxford Martin School
- The Future of Jobs Report, The World Economic Forum
- Boosting transferable skills, Deloitte Insights
- The Future of Work in Technology, Deloitte Insights (Khalid Kark, Bill Briggs, Atilla Terzioglu, Minu Puranik)

Websites

https://futureskills.pearson.com: Look up your job or a job you want and see how safe it is and what skills you will need in the future.

TED talks

- 'Are we headed to a future without jobs?', Martin Ford
- '3 myths about the future of work and why they are not true', Daniel Susskind

Brilliant minds to look up

- Alvin Toffler, writer and futurist
- Maja Korica, Associate Professor of Organisation at Warwick Business School
- Jacob Morgan, author of *The Future of Work*

chapter 3

Are you a human robot?

How do you make frog soup? If you begin with a live frog, you can't just drop it into a pot of boiling water because it will jump out. You need to put the frog in a pan of room temperature water and raise the temperature of the water slowly enough, so the frog doesn't notice it's being cooked. As the water gradually heats up, the frog will sink into a serene stupor, exactly like one of us in a hot bath, and before long, with a smile on its face, it will unresistingly allow itself to be boiled to death.

Granted this is a macabre and well-known story, but it's a good metaphor for how we are losing our humanness and becoming more like human robots. It is slowly creeping up on us so we are hardly noticing it so bit by bit we are losing a lot of our opportunities to be human. Here are a few examples:

- **Dating through apps:** It can all be done and dusted before we have a chance to connect in person.

- **Automated service:** Checkouts, ordering, check-in, pay at pump – we can avoid talking to anyone even when out and about shopping.

- **Online shopping:** You can get all your groceries and Christmas presents without having to leave your home or talk to anyone.

- **Email:** Difficult conversations, selling to customers and talking to colleagues. This is becoming the norm.

The differences between human and human robot

Human robot	Real human
Perfect and rehearsed	Flawed
Emotionless	Emotional
Detached	Empathic
Cold	Compassionate
Apathetic	Curious
Invincible	Vulnerable
Unimaginative	Imaginative
Process led	Creative
Factual	Story-teller
Closed	Open
Unconscious	Aware
Insincere	Authentic

- **Zoom and teams:** Replacing meetings and face-to-face training and education.
- **Social media:** Replacing real socialising.

The human robot quiz

Next is a quiz designed to wake you up and stop you becoming a human robot without realising it. After you have completed it you will be much more conscious of your own behaviour and actions, whilst being more aware of the people around you. It will literally wake up the human in you. Read through it all as there will be bits that will resonate despite your answers. So, for example, if your answers are mostly a), read the narrative for b), c) and d) as well.

The quiz will help you understand where you need to work the hardest and also help you identify areas of strength, equally important.

There are four multiple choice questions to answer for each of the six parts:

1 Unplugged human or dependent robot?

2 Engage – How is your ability to connect and socialise?

3 Listen – Are you just hearing or actively listening?

4 Empathise – Detached robot or warm human?

5 Collaborate – Are you making the most from your work colleagues?

6 Inspire – What story are you telling?

The quiz has been written specifically for this book to give you a snapshot, but if I were you I would want to look at a more in-depth questionnaire and diagnostic tool on the website www.humanworks-academy.co.uk Here you can do a digital test and get your own personalised report. This report will give you more information on your personality type, communication style and the blocks and challenges you will need to work through.

Part 1: Unplugged human or dependent robot?

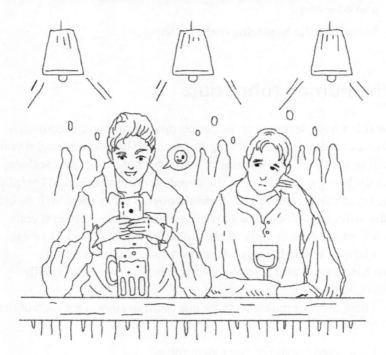

Answer the questions honestly and choose the answer closest to what you would do in most situations.

1 In a normal day, how many screen hours approximately do you use your phone or iPad?
   (a) More than six hours
   (b) More than four hours
   (c) Less than three hours
   (d) Less than one hour

2 You're on your way to meet some friends and realise you have left your phone at home. Do you?
   (a) Immediately turn around and go home to get it even though you are over half way there

(b) Decide it's fine, you won't miss it and then feel anxious about it all night and worry about what you're missing so you don't really enjoy yourself

(c) Think it's a good opportunity to live without it but find yourself looking for it while you're out

(d) Try to leave your phone at home when you go out with friends

3 When do you look at your phone in the morning?
   (a) I don't wait until the morning – if I wake up I will check and see what is going on
   (b) I need my phone for the alarm and when it goes off I may as well check
   (c) Within half an hour to check in with emails, social media, etc
   (d) I usually make a conscious effort to have my phone nowhere near my bedroom

4 How many social media accounts do you have?
   (a) I've lost count probably all of them
   (b) More than five
   (c) Between three and five
   (d) Three or less

Mostly a)

Oh dear! It seems you have a real addiction to your phone and you may be in denial. The first thing is to want to get this more under control. Remind yourself how important real communication is. Not only does spending so much time on your phone erode your conscious human skills, it will also damage relationships over time and could leave you isolated. Set yourself some boundaries: start by limiting the number of hours on your phone and set yourself small targets to try and get it to around three hours.

Leave your phone in the car or in a bag when you are out with family and friends and get yourself an old-fashioned alarm so you can leave your phone downstairs when you go to bed. That way you have to at least get up before you check in with social media.

Mostly b)

You are a little bit addicted to your phone and social media and I think you know it. There is some anxiety when you don't have the phone and you may find yourself being told off by people close to you that you are on your phone too much at the expense of your relationships. Keep an eye on your screen hours. There are lots of ways to keep tabs now and limit yourself. Try to have periods of time where you don't have your phone with you when it feels safer to do so. You could leave it upstairs when you are relaxing with your family or eating a meal. Go a whole day without it at a weekend or take a phone holiday for a few days, where you are only allowed to check in a couple of times a day.

Mostly c)

You have a really nice balance of using the advantages of digital communication and staying in touch with your human side. To maintain this, keep an eye on your screen hours and your level of anxiety around your phone. Give yourself unplugged holidays, like going all weekend without social media or go somewhere where you know the phone signal will be bad.

Mostly d)

You are working hard to keep a control over your digital communication. This is conscious and you are probably aware of how easy it is to find yourself using it in an unhealthy way. Keep a check of the hours you are using your devices so you don't get complacent. This is where I would put myself and I know that if I don't watch it all the time it starts to creep back up.

Top tips on how to be more unplugged

- Take a social media holiday, or delete one of them for a month and see if you miss it.
- Set time limits – there are apps that limit your use to a set number of hours.

- Put some distance between you and your phone – leave it downstairs when you're upstairs or upstairs when you're downstairs.
- Don't take your phone into meetings.
- Turn off your notifications.
- Set yourself goals on how often you look at your phone. Start with every 15 minutes, then 30, 45 and work your way up to 60 minutes if you can. Set an alarm for the times so you don't keep checking on the time. (You may want to let people know about where you are so they don't worry.)
- Take distracting apps off your home screen. Put the ones you feel are most useful such as those for reading or learning something. We often go from one app to the next unconsciously – I tend to look at Facebook, then the weather, then Twitter and back to the weather (it's not likely to change in 15 minutes).
- Leave your phone in a pocket or bag when you go out with friends or family.
- Set some rules with your friends and family and work colleagues to give you all some time off so you can concentrate on each other.
- Go for a walk in the woods where there is no signal, or turn off your devices on the train. Let yourself be a bit bored – it's great for creativity as this is often when we get the sparks of an idea.

Part 2: Engage – how is your ability to connect and socialise?

1 When you're in a bar or coffee shop on your own do you?
    (a) Reach for your phone and catch up with texts, emails, social media
    (b) You're ok for a few minutes and then you reach for your phone

    (c) Enjoy your own company, people-watch and let the time pass

    (d) Start a conversation with someone near you or with a member of staff

2 On a good day when in a place full of people, such as a train, bus, lift or waiting room, which do you want to do?

    (a) Look for a space with the least amount of people, keep your eyes down and reach for your phone, laptop or book – anything to stop people engaging with you

    (b) Acknowledge the people with a nod or fleeting eye contact and a smile and then find a quite spot to sit and look at your phone, laptop or book

    (c) Make eye contact with someone, say hello and make a few minutes of small talk about the weather or something similar

    (d) Make eye contact with someone and engage them in conversation, asking them questions and get totally involved in the conversation if they are up for it

3 When someone comes to your desk what is the most likely outcome?

    (a) Try to ignore them and hope they go away

    (b) Carry on with what you are doing on your PC and talk to them at the same time as you are good at multi-tasking

    (c) Give them eye contact, but you're really thinking about what you were doing, and don't really hear what they are saying

    (d) Tell them you are right in the middle of something and will come and find them in a few minutes, and then do it

4 When it comes to engaging with strangers which of the following is most like you?

    (a) I feel uncomfortable for whatever reason and would prefer to keep myself to myself

    (b) I don't want to be rude and I will engage on the surface but find the whole chitchat stuff uncomfortable and unnatural

    (c) I will engage with strangers if I feel safe, but often find the conversation a bit stilted or I talk too much

    (d) I love meeting new people and am curious about them and their story, and I always give people time but only if that's what they want

Mostly a)

These answers point to the human robot part of us that wants to shut down and be detached. We are social animals but the socialising is often limited to people we are close to, and when it comes to strangers we can be less bold and more 'shy'.

I feel your pain, as it can be really hard to engage with people and make yourself vulnerable enough to share, especially if they are strangers or you don't know them very well. I am a trainer and speaker and can talk to audiences of 300 to 400 people but still feel shy connecting to a stranger on the train.

The good thing is you can learn techniques to make this easier, which is what the masterclass is all about, and you never know you might even start to enjoy it. If you want to work in a customer-facing job such as hospitality or retail or you have aspirations to lead people, the ability to engage naturally is essential. Even if you are involved in technology, as you read in Chapter 2, social skills will be extremely important in the future of work.

Mostly b)

These answers suggest you may have convinced yourself it doesn't matter about socialising with strangers as long as you are engaging with the people that matter the most (I'm only guessing this because I think it myself sometimes). Although it's true that most of your effort should be with your important relationships at home and at work, you still need to flex these muscles regularly other-wise they stop working. Engaging on a human level is important when working in a more transient environment. Employers are looking for people who can connect quickly with team members, customers and suppliers and it's something they will look for in interviews.

Mostly c)

These answers are an indication that you lack some tools to help you take the conversations to a more meaningful level. You don't have a problem in the initial engagement but might find yourself talking too much or it feels stilted and unnatural. The masterclass will be great in helping you to find more authentic ways to engage and build relationships with your work colleagues now and in the future.

Mostly d)

Engaging with others, whether they are strangers or people you know less well, is a strength of yours. You are the sort of person I love to sit next to on a train, someone warm and interested. You make it easier for people like me to engage and feel comfortable. You can develop this ability further in the masterclass by participating in the stretch exercises. Developing this strength can help with some of the other skills such as inspire and collaboration.

The train guard

I was on my way to a training job in London on my usual 7.31am train out of Milton Keynes, and over the public address system the train guard introduced himself and said he was going to give an aerobics class and we could all join in if we wanted.

I know what you are thinking and I thought the same too. But it was so out of the blue it made everyone look up from their phones and laptops. There was a certain amount of cynicism – let's face it, this is not the norm. Even I wondered how many times had he done this. What kept me listening and in the end won us all round was how warm, authentic and brave he was.

He then said he was coming round to check tickets and meet us all and when he arrived he was exactly how he sounded – awake, human and authentic. He chatted to people and they laughed and responded and when he left the carriage you heard people saying 'He's a character' and 'That's different from the normal grumpy ticket inspectors'. A strange thing that happened once he had left was that people in the carriage started talking to each other, only for a few minutes but we all seemed to come alive.

As we were drawing into the station he came over the speaker again to give a shout out to some young people going to Buckingham Palace to receive their Duke of Edinburgh award and wishing them well. The whole of my carriage broke out in applause – it was fantastic.

It was human and it really made a difference. In the future as trains become self-operated, the humans on board will need to have exceptional human skills and these will hopefully be as recognised as much as the technical and engineering roles.

Part 3: Listen – Are you just hearing or actively listening?

1 When you're listening, how much do you think you take in, bearing in mind the UK average is 20% and the maximum for an excellent listener is 70%?
   (a) 15%
   (b) 20%
   (c) 45%
   (d) Above 60%

2 When you're on a video conference call with a number of people and you each have to introduce yourself, when others are doing it do you…?
   (a) Switch of completely and think about what you will say
   (b) Keep an ear out for anything useful but entertain yourself with thinking about other things
   (c) Try to stay focused but find yourself drifting away and getting distracted
   (d) Work hard to stay present and in the moment and if you start to wander remind yourself to remain focused

3 When someone is talking about their holiday, which answer is most likely?
   (a) Think 'Oh no, this is going to be boring. How can I get away?'
   (b) Say 'I've just got back from holiday' and start to tell your story
   (c) You listen and ask questions and find yourself talking about something else in the end
   (d) You ask lots of questions and they really did have an amazing holiday

4 How good are you at multi-tasking while listening?
   (a) I find it really easy as I don't let listening distract me from what I am doing
   (b) I'm a very busy person so multi-tasking is a must unless they are important
   (c) Sometimes I have to multi-task because I am busy but try not to because I don't want to seem rude
   (d) I really struggle with multi-tasking when people are talking about something important as I want to give them my full attention

Mostly a)

Note that this applies, no matter what your answers were.

Research shows that the average person uses only 20% of their listening ability, but as a rule of thumb you should be using 70% of yours. The brain is capable of absorbing words at four or five times the average speed of speech. This leaves 'unused time', which means you will be doing some of the following all or some of the time and are not totally aware of it:

- Judging, evaluating, agreeing or disagreeing with the speaker before they have finished speaking.

- Paying 'fake attention' while in fact occupying the mind with other subject matter, thinking ahead, etc.

- Being impatient, leading to misperception or interruption.

- Letting in external distractions.

- Filtering information imposed by emotion, technical bias, etc.

- Thinking you can multi-task and be unaware of the effect it is having on your listening.

You will also have learned techniques to disguise the fact that you are not really listening properly. The most obvious is the 'nodding dog syndrome' (remember those endlessly nodding dogs in the back of the car in front). You will say encouraging things like 'Yes', 'Mmm', 'Interesting', 'Ah!', 'Absolutely' and so on. If you are a very clever fake, you will repeat back the last part of the last sentence that was spoken. This is all human robot behaviour.

Mostly b)

You are more aware that what you are doing isn't really listening and you probably listen effectively when you think it is important. If you want to be the sort of person people respect and like, see that as your end goal for giving your listening skills more energy and importance. Use the masterclass to re-motivate you and increase your chances of being a better listener. It is just as important as speaking and maybe even more important.

Mostly c)

Even though you value listening and know how important it is, you still find it understandably difficult. You will find the Listening week in the masterclass really helpful to give you tools and techniques to make your life easier and if you commit to the work it will become much more natural.

Mostly d)

You're a great listener because you understand its value. If you skipped the first comment for Mostly a), read it now to remind yourself of the natural human challenges we all have when listening. This is an extremely valuable skill to have and just like top sportspeople it's something that needs constant attention to keep you at your peak of fitness.

Part 4: Empathise – Detached robot or empathetic human?

1 How important do you think empathy is in the workplace?
   (a) I know it has value but I can't help but think feelings shouldn't come into work
   (b) More so if you work in nurturing professions such as nursing or customer service

(c) It's important, people need to care about each other

(d) Essential, it's the lifeblood of a business for the employees and also for the customers to understand how people feel and what they need

2 When a work colleague comes to you with a personal problem, what do you do?

(a) Try to avoid getting into it as I am uncomfortable with people's personal problems

(b) Give them advice and want to solve their problem

(c) Listen for ways I can identify with them and share my own experiences

(d) Listen without judgment, asking questions to get the full picture, making sure they feel really heard, and if I can help I will

3 When showing empathy which of these is your style?

(a) I make sure they know how sorry I am for them

(b) I try to say things like 'I understand' and 'I feel your pain'

(c) I put myself in their shoes and feel their pain, and I find myself getting upset as well

(d) I listen and ask questions to understand how they are feeling, looking for ways to help them if I can

4 When you're having a discussion with someone with very different opinions, what do you do?

(a) Put my view across forcefully especially if I know I am right

(b) Debate with them, listening for opportunities to prove they are wrong

(c) Ask questions to understand where they are coming from and then try to counter their argument

(d) Be really curious to see other's perspective and ask lots of questions as it's a great opportunity to learn and understand people

Mostly a)

You probably struggle with empathy in the workplace, perhaps because you don't have the time or it seems too touchy-feely for you. Your answers also suggest a certain amount of discomfort around empathising, and this can be because you are driven by your head and prefer logical solutions to problems.

Empathy can show a deep respect for co-workers and that you care, as opposed to just going by rules and regulations. If you lead people, empathy can make everyone feel like a team and has been proven to increase productivity.

Most of us have customers of some type, whether they are internal or external, and empathy is critical to understand where your customers are coming from and their needs. If you have any input in product design, marketing, selling, or are involved closely with an entrepreneur, without empathy you could find yourself losing touch with your customers.

Mostly b)

You are confusing empathy for sympathy and think words of kindness will placate most people. You may also find it difficult to let go of your own viewpoint or experiences and end up solving people's problems for them. This is probably coming from the right intentions so with a bit of re-focus and self-awareness you will be able to work at switching these good intentions to empathy when it's appropriate.

Mostly c)

Great, you value empathy and probably feel very deeply for people and do your best to understand how they are feeling. In the masterclass you will learn more about different types of empathy and the bit that's missing for you is the moving beyond stepping into others' shoes and understanding enough so you can find appropriate ways to help and support them. Also, be careful because feeling others' emotions deeply can be overwhelming and damaging after a while.

Mostly d)

Wow, you're the sort of person I need around when I am feeling stressed and overwhelmed. You know how important it is to listen empathetically as opposed to simply putting yourself in their shoes. Your curiosity to want to learn about other perspectives and viewpoints means you are always open to learning and you are able to let go of wanting to be right.

Empathy is a fantastic strength to have and if you can maintain and build on this you will have a valuable and sought-after skill that you can transition across different careers, teams and employers.

The business case for empathy

Empathy is having a comeback and deservedly so. In health-care, research is being carried out that proves empathy saves lives and patients need less drugs and pain killers if they are treated with compassion. People are more likely to go to the doctors and get medical help quickly if they are treated well. There is now so much proof that empathy pays that the NHS is investing in empathy training for doctors and nurses.

In business there are obvious benefits. If we empathise with customers we are more likely to develop products and ser-vices that will sell, and it also encourages customer loyalty and recommendations.

Ryanair is a good example of how it got it completely wrong, but then with its 'Always getting better' programme it was able to turn things around. Most people who flew Ryanair shared stories about seating issues, hidden charges and carry-on luggage restrictions. But in 2015 it started to make changes and the result was a net profit increase from €867 million in the year ending March 2015 to €1.24 billion ($1.39 billion) in the year ending March 2016. CEO Michael O'Leary said infa-mously, 'If I'd only known being nice to customers was going to work so well, I'd have started many years ago.'

For you personally, understanding and developing empathy will make you a better team player, leader and colleague, not to mention the personal benefits of improving your personal close relationships. Robots don't have empathy, so a sure fire way to avoid being a human robot is to develop this skill.

Part 5: Collaborate – Are you making the most of your work colleagues?

1 What is your most likely way of communicating with colleagues at work?
   (a) Usually when we have to in meetings, etc
   (b) Mostly email as it's quick and easy and they might be busy and I don't want to disturb them
   (c) Phone or email, whichever is more appropriate
   (d) As much as possible face to face or on a video conference call

2 What is the most important way to develop collaboration in a team?
   (a) Introduce some sort of cross-communication software system such as Trello or Samepage
   (b) Make sure there are clear boundaries and everyone knows what is expected of them
   (c) Improve communication and understanding, socialise and deal with conflicts
   (d) Have a strong sense of purpose, create ways of working together and understand our strengths as a team, plus all of the ways suggested above

3 How do you give feedback to your colleagues?
   (a) It's not my job to give feedback to my colleagues so I would let the manager do that
   (b) I would be direct and tell them what they are doing wrong and why they should put it right
   (c) I hate giving feedback so I would probably find ways round it and hope it went away
   (d) I would let them know what's working for me and offer suggestions to improve what we are both doing

4 How would you describe a high-performing team or group of people?
   (a) I don't really know as it's not something I have thought about
   (b) One that gets results and everyone knows their role

(c) One that is harmonious without too much conflict, with good communication between team members

(d) One that works effectively together towards a common purpose where everyone feels valued

Mostly a)

You may find it challenging working as part of a team and might find it easier to communicate via an intranet or agile software system, but this type of collaboration is only part of the picture. One of the biggest factors that contributes to the success of any business is whether or not its employees are able to perform together as a team. With increasing competition, it has become extremely important to encourage creativity in a team, in order to improve productivity and promote healthy employee relationships.

It's important that you start to work on your collaboration and teamworking skills as increasingly teams are less stable and you may find yourself moving teams more often. Software programs can be extremely useful for remote working but are no substitute for good communication, understanding and healthy conflict. If you are working remotely choose face-to-face video conferencing over email and most importantly turn your video on, it has been proven that people listen more to people they can see and have eye contact with.

Mostly b)

Your answers suggest you are very task-focused and want to get things done. You might sometimes be too direct or even brutal in your feedback, which is fine for you but think about the impact it has on others, their wellbeing and morale.

It's a good thing to keep things out in the open but it can still be done with empathy and compassion. People are more likely to stay with a business when they have strong connections and relationships with the people they work with and feel they are a part of something bigger. Collaborating isn't easy for everyone, but the benefits are worth making the effort to improve. Read the benefits of collaboration below.

Mostly c)

You value being in a team and harmony is really important to you, which is great, but you might find yourself burying your head in the sand sometimes and putting other people's rights and needs before your own. This can build resentment and may result in passive–aggressive behaviour, which is the enemy of collaboration and teamwork. Pay particular attention to the exercises on dealing with conflict and giving feedback in the masterclass as they will really help you. Read the benefits of collaboration below.

Mostly d)

You understand the value of good teamwork and collaboration and it's important to you to be honest and open and deal with conflict in a constructive way. Teams of the future need people like you because you will be a positive influence on others. You will enjoy the week on collaboration in the masterclass because it gives you great tools to develop a collaborative culture.

Workspace not workplace!

Since the coronavirus working from home is the new normal for a lot of us. During this time, I found myself doing all of my training on Zoom with people joining from their homes. Businesses learnt that their people could be even more productive and could be trusted to get on with their work without the structure of the office. Employees enjoyed not having to do the stressful and often long commute and being able to spend more time with their families.

Flexible working is a great thing for many reasons, but it comes at a cost and if we're not careful it could have serious downsides. Obviously, it's easier to create a collaborative team with more shared dialogue if people are in the same place. Teams need to spend time together to build trust and learn to value and understand each other's strengths, and if they don't some people can feel isolated and lonely, or feel they're missing out.

Being able to have virtual meetings from home in your pyjamas is extremely convenient. I think the Zoom meeting and video-conferencing software is the best thing ever, and I have done all of my interviews for this book with it. But I soon realised you have to work even harder at the social and rapport-building skills. To use this type of technology well means we have to be more human, not less.

If you picture the working environment in the future, chances are we will be working globally across different time zones and the traditional team all working together in the same place at the same time is unlikely. Technology is going to be used more and more to collaborate. That's great as I'm all for saving the planet by not having to fly all the way to Australia for work, but we need to find ways to keep the real human connection. Working from home and using technology isn't a bad thing, but it does mean we have to work a little harder to collaborate and build relationships, whatever the medium, and make the most of any face-to-face time.

Benefits of collaboration and teamwork

- **Share talents and strengths:** When members of a team collaborate, they are able to use the knowledge, experience and skills of everyone concerned.

- **Improve skills:** Collaboration is equally useful for employees as well as the business because when we work together, interact and share ideas, we see and understand how others work, think, negotiate and function. This gives everyone a chance to pick up skills from colleagues and teammates and build upon their strengths.

- **Speed up results:** Collaboration speeds things up. It advances progress. A problem that may take months to get resolved when handled by a single individual may take just a few hours to resolve when a team employs its unique viewpoints and knowledge to get things done. This will open up several doors to numerous ideas and solutions that a single individual may not be able to come up with.

- **Boost employee retention and job satisfaction:** Collaboration brings meaning and adds value to the way team members see their job. Because of this, they feel good about what they do. The sense of team spirit is felt most strongly when victories can be shared.

Part 6: Inspire – What story are you telling?

1 What's more important when influencing someone: facts and data, or stories that connect emotionally?
   (a) I know that I'm supposed to say stories but I struggle telling them
   (b) Data and facts are really important and sometimes stories can be irritating
   (c) It would depend on the person and what they need
   (d) A story is a great way to serve up facts and data in a memorable way

2 You have a great idea so how would you attempt to sell it to your boss?
   (a) I would tell them how great it was and not take no for an answer, offering a compelling argument
   (b) I would prepare well and present a logical, factual argument
   (c) I would do some research on what is important to them right now and try to link my idea to that so it helps them as well
   (d) I would do the above and then paint a picture of how my idea would make a difference

3 'Treat people the way you want to be treated?' How do you feel about this related to inspiring others?
   (a) Absolutely true and it's what we should all strive for
   (b) It's good advice most of the time but it doesn't always work
   (c) Shouldn't it be 'Treat people the way they want to be treated'
   (d) Its ok if you are talking about a moral code but not for influencing, as you need to understand someone and what's important to them if you want to have any chance of doing it well

4 What's more important when presenting: preparation or delivery?

    (a) Definitely delivery – if you're a good presenter you can wing it

    (b) As long as you have slides to prompt you, then I think delivery is more important

    (c) They are both important and I can't choose between them

    (d) It's true they are both important but I would say preparation, because you can't deliver effectively if you don't understand your audience and rehearsal is essential for great delivery

Mostly a)

This is important for everyone to read.

When you have an idea you feel strongly about, you will probably talk about it with passion and conviction, telling anyone you are trying to influence what a brilliant idea it is. Your preference is for facts and detail but this might not be everyone else's preference. It's important to understand how different types of people want to receive information.

Influencing isn't just about having belief and conviction for something. That's just half of it, and the other half is finding out more about the person or people you are influencing and persuading so you can help them see how any idea would be of value to them. People are swayed by what is in it for them as well as being moved by someone's energy and passion.

You are missing a trick when it comes to storytelling, as there are solid scientific reasons why stories influence, persuade and inspire people more than facts and data on PowerPoint slides. Stories in business don't have to be fluffy and emotional. It depends on your audience, but even if they are logical types putting the facts and data into a story makes it more powerful and memorable and engages different parts of the brain.

We are not robots – we are human and we connect more to a human story because we are wired that way. The masterclass will give you tools and techniques to help you be more successful when you want to get people on your side.

Read the case for storytelling below for more evidence on why stories work.

Mostly b)

You are influencing mostly by telling as above and probably push your ideas forward with key facts and details, but you are more aware that there is something missing. And there is. Humans don't buy facts, they buy value and how it impacts on them. It's just as important to understand your audience and their needs and wants as it is to believe strongly in your proposal. The masterclass will help you to be more aware of your audience and how to sell value rather than cold, dry facts.

You are also missing a very powerful tool if you don't include storytelling in your skillset, so read the case for storytelling below.

Mostly c)

You instinctively know that understanding the people you want to influence and persuade is critical if you want to get them on your side. You also appreciate that there is a balance between taking the time to find out what they value and being passionate and convincing in how you put ideas forward. You have probably read about storytelling and how important it is but are a little unsure on how to capitalise on using it and feel uncomfortable telling stories in business. The masterclass will help to develop your skills further and turn you into a master influencer.

Mostly d)

You already appreciate the art of influencing. Maybe you are in a sales career of some sort or you are a business owner who understands only too well the importance of understanding customer needs. You put a lot of importance on research and preparation, which means your case will be stronger as a result, but don't forget to hold fast to your belief and conviction for an idea.

Don't skip the Inspire section of the masterclass because it will be right up your street and will give you a chance to test and refine your influencing skills.

Read the case for storytelling below as I think you will find it interesting.

The business case for storytelling

Storytelling has the power to engage, influence, teach and inspire listeners. That's why I wanted to include it in this book. There's an art to telling a good story, and we all know a good story when we hear one. But there's also a science behind the art of storytelling.

We have all had to endure long and boring PowerPoint presentations with slides full of bullet points that are of no use to us the audience but are a prompt to the presenter, proving they didn't care enough to rehearse. Even if they are a brilliant and charismatic speaker it's hard to engage with information when it's delivered this way.

When we deliver the same facts within a story there is research that proves more than just the language part of our brain is activated. Stories are able to transport us; we can feel for the characters and the situation without having to live it ourselves. Business stories will be less emotional and dramatic, but as a customer nothing is more persuasive than hearing about other people similar to us who have had their lives improved as a result of a product or service we are about to buy.

There are also additional scientific elements at play. Scientists are discovering that chemicals like cortisol, dopamine and oxytocin are released in the brain when we're told a story. Why is this important? If we are trying to make a point stick in our mind, cortisol assists with our formulating memories. Dopamine, which helps regulate our emotional responses, keeps us engaged. When it comes to creating deeper connections with others, oxytocin is associated with empathy, an important element in building, deepening or maintaining good relationships.

Perhaps most importantly, storytelling is central to things making sense. We are able to process and learn from the information quicker and easier, which is why we always learn from stories, and humans have been doing this since the cave paintings. Remember even in a straightforward business presentation, a story helps to illustrate a point better than a set of facts. A story gives people a reason to care about what you're saying. They relate to the characters, the plot and the lessons learned. They relate to your story, and therefore your message.

Now that you have completed the quiz, give yourself a score for each question in each section using the table below. Note that the scoring for each part is slightly different.

Make some comments on any specifics you think are important for you to take into account before you start working on your roadmap. When you move on to the masterclass I would recommend you complete all the exercises because even if you scored highly in some areas there are some great tools to help you maximise these strengths.

Highlight the areas where you have scored lowest, as these are the areas you need to pay special attention to and may mean more work.

Sections	Total score	Comment
Part 1: Unplugged human **(a)** answers – score 1 each **(b)** answers – score 3 each **(c)** answers – score 7 each **(d)** answers –score 10 each		
Part 2: Engage **(a)** answers – score 1 each **(b)** answers – score 3 each **(c)** answers – score 7 each **(d)** answers – score 10 each		

Sections	Total score	Comment
Part 3: Listen **(a)** answers – score 1 each **(b)** answers – score 1 each **(c)** answers – score 7 each **(d)** answers – score 10 each		
Part 4: Empathise **(a)** answers – score 1 each **(b)** answers – score 2 each **(c)** answers – score 5 each **(d)** answers – score 10 each		
Part 5: Collaborate **(a)** answers – score 1 each **(b)** answers – score 1 each **(c)** answers – score 7 each **(d)** answers – score 10 each		
Part 6: Inspire **(a)** answers –score 1 each **(b)** answers – 1 each **(c)** answers – score 7 each **(d)** answers – score 10 each		

Don't forget you can get a more detailed digital questionnaire and personalised report at our website www.humanworksacademy.co.uk

chapter 4

Use your roadmap to stand out

People talk about personal brand and even write books about it, but I think we should talk about our human brand instead and this chapter will help you discover it. A human brand is very different from corporate branding. Using Guinness as an example, we think of the product's identity, its market positioning and its core message. When I talk about creating your human brand I mean understanding your core strengths, building on them, knowing what makes you stand out and telling your story to inspire the people around you. This includes how you're perceived at work and in interviews for a promotion or a new job. It's all very well having a human brand, but if people are not seeing or believing it, then you are not standing out so what's the point.

In the last chapter you completed the Human robot quiz (if you haven't taken this yet, go back and complete it now). This will have given you some evidence to build your roadmap to humanness and will be your guide, helping you focus on the areas most important to you when you do the masterclass that follows. Now is the time to reach for that journal I asked you to buy. It's now really going to come into its own.

Exercise 1
Developing a growth mindset

- -

Open your journal and being really honest write down your answers to the following questions:

1 When you see or hear about someone else's success, how does it make you feel? Does it make you feel you're not doing enough? If so, why?

2 Does the success of others threaten you, or make you feel uncomfortable, and in what way?

3 If something's difficult and outside your comfort zone, do you find yourself giving up when it gets tough? How does this feel?

4 When you're trying to be successful at something, do you try avoiding failure at all costs? Why?

5 When you fail, do you see it as confirmation you're not good at something, or don't have the intelligence to succeed at it?

6 Do you resist challenges if they make you feel uncomfortable? Why?

7 Do you find critical feedback difficult to take and try to ignore it? How does it make you feel?

- -

If you answered yes to any of the questions above, you have a fixed mindset in some parts of your life and you need to do some work on your growth mindset. Even if your answers are all positive, it's still something that needs constant maintenance. Let me explain.

What is a growth mindset?

This growth mindset is based on the belief that your basic qualities are things you can cultivate through your efforts, your strategies, and help from others. Although people

may differ in every which way—in their initial talents and aptitudes, interests, or temperaments—everyone can change and grow through application and experience.

Carol Dweck

If you have children at school, the chances are you'll have come across growth mindset, being a theory developed to help children and students understand how they can be more successful with their learning. Professor Carol Dweck from Stanford University in the US developed this powerful theory; she spent decades researching the field of achievement and success, coming up with a new psychology of success based on mindset. More and more, this theory is being used to help adults too, whether you're an entrepreneur or work for someone else. Applying this theory can be life-changing and set you apart from others.

Growth mindset versus fixed mindset

Carol Dweck's research looks at people's abilities and talents from two different viewpoints, showing that you can have a different mindset towards different things in your life. For example, I've a growth mindset when it comes to the delivery of my training and a fixed mindset when it comes to learning new software or technology. It's no accident that I'm successful with my training and totally useless with technology.

- **Fixed mindset:** Your intelligence is fixed and you can't change it. Challenges are avoided, as failure equals lack of ability, so effort is seen as fruitless. Getting things wrong and receiving feedback is negative and damaging, because it shows you up as having limitations.

- **Growth mindset:** Your intelligence can be developed and challenges are welcomed because you believe it's all about improvement. Effort is worthwhile to becoming a master of something. Making mistakes and getting feedback is therefore positive as it develops improvement and growth.

When I deliver any type of leadership training, I always start with a session on growth mindset, because, without it, a lot of learning can excite you for a few days (or weeks, if you're lucky), but then have no real impact on your success or change your behaviour. I've lost count of the number of self-help books I've read, where I've been inspired and enthused by the ideas, only to give up after the first challenge or setback. Understanding the importance of growth mindset, versus a fixed mindset, will be the difference, whether this book changes your life or ends up in your loft.

You might not be into football, but I am sure you'll have heard of Cristiano Ronaldo, one of the greatest footballers playing today (I'm an Arsenal fan myself so this is an unbiased opinion). Of course, he has natural talent and abilities, but his mother famously said she didn't think he was that good. What Ronaldo does have is a growth mindset, so he was prepared to put in the extra effort and listen to the people he believed were better than him and who were prepared to help him perfect his talent. It turned him into one of the best players to ever have kicked a football. His former teammates at Manchester United said he was always the first and last person on the training field, perfecting his technical skills. He was heard to say 'I only want to train with the best, so I can become the best.'

You'll find some areas where you have a natural talent – maybe you're a good speaker or storyteller, or maybe you're more intro-verted and find listening actively to people comes naturally. Imagine if you adopted a Cristiano Ronaldo growth mindset to these natural abilities; you could become a master storyteller or even a master listener. Equally, if there's an area that doesn't come so easily, such as meeting strangers and starting a conversation, running a collab-orative team meeting, or being able to focus on asking questions to understand, rather than to reply. Instead of saying, 'That's not my thing, it's just not me' or 'I'll never be able to do that', try applying a growth mindset to it. You could get better, become more confident, or even be an expert.

Top tip

If you have a growth mindset, you:

- believe that intelligence can be developed
- are persistent and embrace challenges
- know that effort can help you master anything
- learn from criticism
- find lessons and inspiration in the success of others
- welcome challenges and view setbacks as an opportunity to learn and grow.

The great news is you can change your mindset. Even reading this book should start you thinking and reacting in a more growth mindset way. For example, let's say there are two marketing consultants on a team, one with a fixed mindset and one with a growth mindset. The fixed mindset marketer will be more likely to stick to 'business as usual'. They will use techniques and methods they know have worked in the past, and will be averse to trying new things because they want to rely on their talents alone.

The growth mindset marketer, on the other hand, believes the best work comes from trying new solutions. They will be more likely to search out opportunities to test new and forward-looking ideas, without fearing they won't be good at it right away (and it will take work). It might not be the right choice, but they'll learn from it anyway and become a better marketer in the long run.

Which one of these marketers stand out? I know which one of these I would rather have on my team and any potential employer would feel the same. It's not a magic wand, but it'll help you be more resilient and more positive, two extremely attractive characteristics for potential employers (or if you're looking for promotion).

Seven ways to develop a growth mindset

1 **Say yes to opportunities to step outside of your comfort zone** In the masterclass, there are going to be lots of opportunities to step outside your comfort zone, as you are given sprint and stretch exercises to do, at least once a day. I encourage you to do the more difficult exercise, even if it makes you feel sick in your stomach. When you're done, reflect on what you learnt and how much you've expanded your comfort zone.

2 **Ask questions – there is no such thing as a stupid question** There's no shame in asking questions to expand your knowledge or understand something better. When you were a child, you never stopped asking questions, so step back in time and be the curious child again.

3 **See challenges as growth opportunities** When you reflect on activities that challenge you, try not to focus on the obstacles and more on how you overcame them. List everything you learnt in the process and see how much you have grown. This will help you embrace challenges as opportunities and chances to learn.

4 **Learn to love your mistakes** We learn more by getting things wrong than in any other way, and yet we often beat ourselves up when we do. If we want to grow, taking risks is essential. If you make a mistake, don't be hard on yourself. Instead, think about how far you have come.

5 **Don't hide from feedback, seek it out instead** I know it's hard to hear criticism and it's easy to get defensive, so as an alternative, why not ask a question, find out more about where it's coming from and by not making it personal, you can look and understand how it can help you. Be brave and seek it out from people you trust (more on this in this chapter).

6 **Reflect, reflect, reflect** This is one of the reasons I have asked you to get a journal because it is the best way to develop your skills. It's about questioning in a positive way

what you did and deciding if there is a better way to do it in the future (more on this too later in the chapter).

7 **Actively seek out new things – the more you do, the more you learn** In the masterclass, you'll be given exercises that mean doing something different and new. My advice is to be brave and go for it, because it literally is 'Who dares wins'.

By asking yourself some key questions, you can turn most experiences into opportunities to learn and grow. This is one of the core skills you will use throughout the five weeks of the masterclass. I'll be reminding you to keep developing your growth mindset, and as an added bonus it is something extra you can add to your new skillset and your ability to stand out from the crowd.

The power of 'not yet'

In Carol Dweck's inspiring TED talk she tells the story of how in one American high school the staff graded their students if they had not passed a subject as 'not yet' rather than a fail. When I first heard that, a light bulb went off for me. If it's not yet that surely means I'm on my way, I'm on a learning curve, a journey, so if I teach my three-year old granddaughter just one thing it will be the power of 'not yet'. This idea opens so many more doors and opportunities in an ever-changing working environment where we will need to be constantly learning. Make the 'not yet' a mantra whenever you are learning new skills and you can literally do anything.

By asking yourself some key questions you can turn most experiences into opportunities to learn and grow, so this is one of the core skills which will be threaded throughout the five weeks of the masterclass. I will remind you to keep developing your growth mindset and this is something else you can add to your new skillset. This is one of the most important ways to stand out in an interview, new job or in your current team. What employer wouldn't want someone with this sort of attitude?

irected learning

...to have an enlightening interview with Garry Goldman, Learning and Development Director for Centrica (British Gas), and he told me how important he thinks self-directed learning is going to be in the future: 'We need people to think bigger picture, more systemically, rather than sitting in silos. I need people who have a much more inquiring, learning mindset instead and who ask lots of questions.'

Garry also told me that people would need to take more responsibility for their own learning and development in the future because with so many changes happening in the world of work it will be hard for businesses to keep up.

'I hate to say it, we are always trying to cut costs across the learning function. Plus, actually, the changes mean I can't keep up with everybody's learning needs to fully enable people to do all the different roles. I need people to come in and say they're hungry for learning and they actually want to grow.'

'We've been employing self-employed contractors in the organisation, and I find that they are far hungrier than full-time employees. It's almost like they're the transient workforce and they know the value of learning. So now, I've got the time and I've got the opportunity, I'm going to suck in as much new knowledge as possible to keep me employable.'

Get feedback, get better

Receiving feedback can be difficult for us because ultimately we are animals and naturally have a negativity bias. This means our brains are hardwired to react to negative stimuluses. This is all because originally it was essential to our survival, and so sensing an attack would trigger our natural default to a fight or flight response, causing us to react much quicker and instinctively to what we perceive to be dangerous. This fear comes from a time when we were part of a hunter-gatherer society and totally dependent on the group for survival, so constructive feedback (a perceived attack) can trigger a fear that we'll no longer be accepted in the tribe.

It's important to be comfortable with asking for and receiving feedback. It will unlock your blind spots, reveal strengths and weaknesses you may not even know you have. And on the positive side, it will give you helpful suggestions on how you could do better. It's been proven that people who seek constructive feedback adapt more quickly to new roles, are higher performers, are seen as more committed to their work and you got it stand out!

My advice is be proactive and ask for feedback. It's much easier to take when it's initiated by you, putting you in control of what you want to receive and who you want to receive it from. Look at my tips below; they explain how to make the most of asking for feedback.

How to ask for feedback

- **Be clear on what you're looking for:** What sort of feedback do you desire? Do you want the positives or the areas for development? Do you want general feedback or feedback on a specific skill or project? Asking for the feedback in the right way gives you what you need and there are no surprises.

- **Don't put it off:** If you need feedback on something specific, say your last presentation, ask for it sooner than later, keep it informal and relaxed, giving some direction on the key areas you're looking for, making it more manageable in smaller chunks. For example, 'How well did I engage with the audience?'

- **Think about questions to ask:** Don't ask 'Have you got any feedback for me?' It's a closed question, so the chances are you will get a no (it's often harder to give feedback than it is to take it). Ask instead something like 'What's one thing I can improve on?' or 'What do you think I could have done differently?' These types of questions are open and make it clear it's about improvement and help, not negative criticism.

- **Ask for examples:** Once you have been given feedback, dig down more for specifics, an example being, 'You said I could have had more energy, so what kinds of things could I have done to have been more energetic? Can you explain more about what you mean?'

- **Cast your net wide:** It doesn't have to be just your boss you ask. You should ask the people that are most affected, in other words, the audience at the presentation or your colleagues who helped you put it together. You can also seek feedback from customers, friends and family. It all depends on what you are looking for.

Exercise 2
Seek feedback

- -

You will have probably guessed by now what I am going to ask you to do and if it makes your stomach turn, I don't blame you. I had the exact same reaction when I did it (of course I won't ask you to do anything I'm not prepared to do myself). I want you to send out an email to elicit feedback from people you trust and respect. Send it to at least ten people, choosing a cross-section of friends, family and colleagues.

I have done this exercise several times and the most recent was just before I started to write this chapter. The first response I had was from the people contacting me to tell me how brave I was and that they would give it some thought and get back to me. A few days later the feedback started to come in. Because I had chosen carefully it was gentle and constructive with really helpful suggestions. Remember too that understanding your strengths is equally important as knowing your weaknesses.

Look for any trends. For example, I was told by several people that when I was tired or distracted it felt to them like I was going through the motions of listening, asking questions but not really being interested in the answers. Since this feedback I have been working hard at being honest and telling people I have zoned out and then re-focusing.

Be prepared. Even if delivered carefully, you are likely to feel defensive. It's our natural first response to constructive feedback. Take a deep breath and accept it might take time to settle. Read it several times and (if needed) ask someone else you trust to read it. You may be reading things into it that aren't there. Feedback reveals your blind spots, which is why it can be extremely disconcerting, unsettling, but ultimately, enormously valuable.

- -

Below is the wording I sent and please feel free to change and amend it to reflect your personality.

Dear friends, family and colleagues

Thank you so much for reading this email. I'm sending it to a select number of people because each of you knows me well, and I'm hoping you will give me honest feedback about my strengths and areas that I could improve on and develop.

Specifically, I am looking for feedback on my human skills: how I engage with people, empathise, listen, collaborate and inspire others. This is not easy for me, but I feel that for me to grow and improve as a person I need to get a more accurate picture of how I'm showing up to the people who matter most to me.

So, all I'm asking is that you take just a few minutes to email me back with what you honestly think are my top two or three areas for improvement and my two or three key strengths. I would love to hear any helpful suggestions.

Thank you again, and if there is anything else I can do to help you please let me know.

[Sign off with your name]

Once you receive your feedback, make a note in your journal of any key themes or anything that resonates with you. How does it compare to your own awareness of yourself? How does it relate to the human robot quiz? This will give you more information to help create your roadmap.

Reflection

Reflect, learn, grow – let it go.

Adam Kreek, Olympic gold medal winner 2008 for rowing and motivational speaker

Self-reflection is exactly what it says on the tin: holding up an imaginary mirror and taking a good look at yourself. It's also a brilliant way to help learning stick. There's not much point in pushing yourself outside your comfort zone without it changing anything. It's about questioning in a positive way what you do and why you do it, giving you the opportunity to decide whether there's a better, or more efficient, way of doing it in the future.

Reflecting daily is the equivalent of a warm-down exercise at the gym, making your journal invaluable as you progress through the masterclass. At the end of each week you'll be asked to reflect with the following questions:

- Did I do something that was out my comfort zone? How did it make me feel?

- What did I learn that would help me achieve my goals?

- How am I changing and what examples have I got that prove this?

- What can I do better or differently next week?

- What was the best thing that happened to me this week?

- What did I discover new about myself?

- What will I keep working on to improve myself?

Don't worry if you're thinking you won't have time. You can still use these questions to reflect without having to write a single word. The key is identifying little pockets of time that are otherwise wasted during the day.

Top tips

- Reflect in bed, either after your alarm has gone off and before you get up, or before you fall asleep at night. It can be an invaluable time to prepare yourself for the day ahead (in the morning), or to process the events of the day (at night).

- In the shower or in the bath is an ideal time for reflection as it may be one of the few chances for real solitude in your day.

- If you have a dog and go for a morning or evening walk this is another perfect time to reflect.

- If you drive to work and find yourself stuck in traffic, take a few minutes to turn off the radio and reflect. If you take public transport, rather than go to your phone, let yourself reflect on the day ahead or on the day you're coming home from for a few minutes.

Exercise 3
Stand out roadmap

- -

Go to our website www.humanworksacademy.co.uk for a roadmap template.

This is where we bring it all together to create your roadmap.
Use your journal to make notes and work through the following questions. Also use the answers from the human robot quiz and your feedback from the previous exercise to help inform your answers. You'll have plenty of opportunity to revisit this throughout the masterclass, so don't worry if you don't have the answers to everything. The point is that it's a living document which will evolve. This is a roadmap to humanness and will help you to re-word your social media profiles, apply for jobs and promotions, tell your story and stand out from all the others.

- -

Know yourself

1 What are your key strengths?

2 What are your main growth areas?

3 What three things can you do to be a more unplugged human?

4 How healthy is your mindset? Give yourself a mark out of 10.

5 What three things can you do to develop a growth mindset?

What do you want people to say about you?

Your real human brand is the story people tell about you when you're not in the room, whether at your present job, or after an interview looking for a new opportunity. To begin, you should consider how you want to show up at work. Answer the two questions below about your human skills (not the work skills you have).

- How do I want people to speak of me at work or describe me to others? Write down at least seven adjectives. For example, curious, compassionate, approachable, conscientious, honest, open, inspiring.

- What do I want to be known for? Write down three sentences. For example:

  - A good listener who asks questions seeking to understand other people's ideas and opinions without an agenda.

  - A kind person willing to help others.

  - A person with interesting ideas who can share their vision in a way to inspire others to follow.

Personal values

Underpinning all of this will be your personal values, beliefs and what you stand for. Understanding what these are will help you find your direction and keep you on track. Answer the following questions:

- What do I stand for? My example: freedom, kindness and compassion, helping others.
- What are my strongest beliefs? My example: justice and everyone's chance to be heard, equality for all.
- How do I define and describe myself? My example: creative, compassionate, vulnerable, mother and wife.
- What words do I want to live by? My example: openness, understanding, courage, curiosity, loyalty, honesty, fairness.

What's your story?

Start creating your story. Some people call it an 'elevator pitch', but I personally believe a story is more human. We'll come back to this in the masterclass, but for now write out what you would say to someone if they asked 'Why you? What can you bring to a job, business or team?'. Later I'll help you to craft this into your story.

Here is an example.

My story

For the last 20 years I have been passionate about helping people be the best people they can be at work. The training workshops I deliver reflect my style, which is warm, energetic, approachable and authentic. I care about people and work hard to be a curious, empathetic listener seeking to understand rather than talk about myself. With my team I encourage ideas and new ways of doing things and try to give everyone a voice. Treating everyone as an equal is very important to me.

I am driven and when I put my mind to something, no matter what the challenges are, I will keep going until I am successful. This has led me to have a life that has been full of challenges and adventures and learning which keeps me motivated with a sense of purpose.

So you now have the beginnings of your human roadmap, which you will be able to add to throughout the masterclass. This will be a fantastic document to help you prepare for interviews or when you have to pitch yourself in anyway and it's always a yardstick for who you want to be.

When it comes to human skills, we need to use them or lose them and now is the time to do the real work. Over the next five weeks, the masterclass that follows will boost your conscious human skills, strengthen your relationships at work and in your personal life, make new connections and develop ways to influence and inspire the people around you. Complete the five weeks of exercises and you will go a long way to standing out in an ever-changing working environment.

Recommended reading and viewing

You can read or watch more about negativity bias and our sense of exclusion by looking up the following on the internet:

- Peter Gray, psychologist: 'Play as a foundation for hunter-gatherer social existence'.
- Short Takes: Neal Ashkanasy on emotions in the workplace.
- Ted talks: Jenni Flinders, Own your personal brand.
- Ted talks: Carol Dweck, The power of believing that you can improve.

part 2

The masterclass

This is it, time to roll up your sleeves and do some work. As I said in Chapter 1, this book is not just a read but an actual course in human skills. I am using the analogy of an exercise masterclass because human skills are physical and just like muscles in our body they need constant working out to keep them firm and fit.

This masterclass runs over five weeks to focus on one of the five key skills each week. There are 25 days with five exercises each day helping you to build positive habits, develop confidence and develop the critical human skills that will make you stand out.

The exercises in the first week will ease you in and then as it builds and you get fitter it will get harder and take you further outside of your comfort zone. It is scary to step outside your comfort zone into the fear zone and your reptilian brain will warn you to stay safe. If you can be brave to step through the fear zone into the learning zone you will be rewarded as this is where you expand your universe and learn the most.

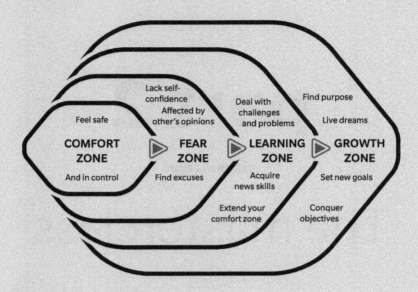

Beyond your comfort zone

Each day there will be five key exercises to complete, as follows:

Warm-up: To get you thinking and improve your self-awareness. This is where I will give you some input on the skills and tools you will put into practice during the sprint and stretch exercises.

Core exercise: Essential exercises that you can do on your own in your journal. They are the more analytical exercises that I teach in my workshops and they will develop your knowledge and prepare you to stretch yourself.

Sprint: Quick and easy exercises that you can use if you can't quite bring yourself to stretch or do both.

 **Stretch:** Challenging, experiential exercises to push you outside your comfort zone.

 **Warm-down:** Reflection and reviewing progress.

Also look out for some virtual alternatives for when close contact isn't possible or appropriate; remember in this new world of connecting it doesn't mean you should leave your humanness at the door.

At the end of each week there will also be a progress check to do over the weekend. This will cover:

- personal reflection in your journal
- revisiting your roadmap to humanness
- setting SMARTER goals.

Try to do the warm-up and core exercises either the day before or the morning of each day so you are ready to take on a sprint and/or a stretch. If you want the best results, do all of the exercises. If we go to the gym it can be tempting to skip the warm-ups and warm-downs but then we suffer the next day.

 At the end of each week there is also a progress check so you can message yourselves against the criteria you set in your roadmap. Don't skip this as it's a critical and fun part of the class – just like a fitness test or weigh-in. Seeing yourself progress is motivational.

chapter 5

Week one: Engage

Your social skills and the ability to connect authentically

Week one, day one

This week is about engaging. Engaging with people should be a natural and instinctive thing. On one level it is, but this is a masterclass so it's not about connecting on a surface level. You will learn with practice and application the skills to become captivating and magnetic. You don't have to be an outgoing extrovert to shine – on the contrary introverts can be equally as engaging in a different way. Barack Obama is a perfect example of an introvert who had you hanging on to every word.

This isn't about acting a part or pretending to be someone you are not. In a recent survey, people were asked which of the following annoyed them the most:

- Someone who is too talkative
- Someone who is too quiet
- Someone who shows off
- Someone who is fake

Being fake won by a mile – 63% – while the next highest, showing off, was 22%. If you are human you are real and vulnerable, which is so much more engaging than fake and perfect. If you watch TED talks the ones that have the most views and resonate with us are polished, but they are also less than perfect and we can tell that the speaker is real.

In week one we are going to work on helping you to connect in a way that's comfortable and natural for you. You will learn things that set you up for the rest of the masterclass where we build on these skills as they connect with one another.

On day one you will learn how to:

- take a temperature check on your working relationships
- be comfortable making quick connections
- use 20 minutes every day to improve your working relationships.

Exercise: Week one, day one
Making connections

- -

Answer the following questions honestly in your journal.

1 Which of these two statements is closest to the way you are thinking and feeling?

   (a) I want to improve my ability to engage and connect and believe with effort I can learn and develop the skills.

   (b) I want to improve my ability to engage and connect but I am nervous about getting started and have doubts about whether it will work or if I am capable of changing.

If your answer is a) that is great as it suggests you have a positive mindset. If your answer is b) remember to use the 'not yet' technique – keep working on the skills, reflect on what you have achieved, learn from mistakes and put the effort in. You might not be there yet but you will be.

2 Which of these two statements is closest to the way you are thinking and feeling?

   (a) I find doing and learning new things stressful and I might avoid anything too far outside of my comfort zone.

   (b) I am ready to push myself outside my comfort zone even if it means making mistakes and not being successful straightaway.

If your answer is b) it suggests you are willing to be brave and take risks to progress. If your answer is a) remember it is ok to feel the fear – it means you are about to make a breakthrough (see figure above).

Think of three work colleagues you have a good connection with and could describe as warm and then three that are less warm (cool). These can be team members, direct reports, people in other departments or even external people such as customers and suppliers.

Fill out the temperature check thermometers below.

Name	Name	Name	Name	Name	Name

Temperature check thermometers

Reflect on why the warm ones are warm and the others are less so. What are you doing differently?

 Pick one of the cool relationships and today find out one thing you have in common with them. The key thing here is to use this to connect but most importantly to ask questions. Make this about them, not you, and be generous with your listening.

To get you started think of asking questions about pets, sports and hobbies, places they have visited or even food you both like.

 Imagine devoting just 20 minutes of every working day to engaging with your work colleagues. That's over 84 hours a year. What a difference you could make. It doesn't have to be all face to face as long as it's dedicated time to engage and improve the connections.

Today pick one of your colleagues from each category – one warm and one less warm – and spend ten minutes on each relationship.

You might like to do one or more of the following:

- Take them for a coffee and stop for a chat.
- Invite them out for lunch or a drink.
- Say thank you in whatever way is appropriate.
- Spend a few minutes to find out what is important to them.
- Pick up the phone and catch up.
- Comment on a LinkedIn post.
- If the relationship is a cool one, what are you doing that has made the other ones warm that might help here.

Virutal alternative – There is nothing to stop you doing any of the above through video conferencing, remember keep it short and sweet but make the effort.

Top tip

Keep a balance. Despite all of the tips above, this relates to work and therefore it should not take over your whole life and damage personal relationships.

Well done! You have made it through your first day. Here is a quick and simple way to reflect and build on what you have achieved called 'Start, stop, continue'.

This exercise is an old favourite based on today's exercises. Write in your journal one thing you will start doing, one thing you will stop doing . . . and one thing you will continue to do.

Week one, day two

On day two you will learn how to:

- recognise different communication styles
- understand what your main communication preference is
- flex to other people's styles.

Exercise: Week one, day two
Knowing me, knowing you

- -

Understanding the different ways of communicating can help a lot when engaging with others, and equally knowing your own style is useful. If you have taken a personality test, such as the Myers–Briggs Type Indicator (MBTi), Insights Discovery or DiSC, you will already be more self-aware. Now you are going to take a very short test which we can expand on in further chapters as it links with all of the key skills.

Read the following statements and tick only the ones that apply to you. There is no right or wrong answer and you may feel as if it depends on the situation but think about what you prefer to do and where you feel most comfortable.

1 When asked a question, I hesitate as I like to think before I speak.

2 When I am asked a question, I give an immediate answer, speaking my thoughts.

3 After spending time with a large group of people at a networking event or a party, I feel tired and drained and want time to myself.

4 After spending time with a large group of people at a networking event or a party I will be buzzing and energised, ready for more.

5 I am seen by others as quiet and reflective.

6 I am seen by others as outgoing and talkative.

7 When I'm working on something I prefer not to be interrupted.

8 When I'm working on something I don't mind a few interruptions as a welcome distraction.

Add up your totals as follows:

- Statements 1, 3, 5 and 7 (introvert) total:
- Statements 2, 4, 6, 8 (extrovert) total:

The behaviour you have most ticks for is the behaviour you are demonstrating more often.

Preferences of introverts	Preferences of extroverts
• Listen more, talk less • Gain energy through inner reflection and solitude • Think through your ideas before you tell them to others • Prefer a few deep, close relationships to many casual ones • Feel tired and drained after socialising, even if you enjoyed it	• Talk more, listen less • Gain energy from socialising and being out and about • Prefer talking with someone rather than sitting alone thinking • Think *as* you speak, so you talk through your ideas • Express yourself well verbally

If you don't know what an extrovert thinks, you haven't been listening. If you don't know what an introvert thinks, you haven't asked them!

Isabel Briggs Myers

 Think of one work colleague who has an introverted preference and one who has an extroverted preference. They can also be external such as an important client. Answer the following questions in your journal:

Which of them do you find easiest to engage with?

Are they the same type as you (introvert or extrovert)?

Who is more difficult to engage with? What could you do differently to make it easier for you both to connect?

Extrovert with introverts

• Take your time and slow your pace.

• Give them space to answer any questions you ask.

• Don't interrupt and be patient.

Introverts with extroverts

- Show energy and enthusiasm when they are talking.
- Ask questions that help them articulate their thoughts.
- Give them verbal nods and open body language to show you are interested.

Be super-aware today of the different types of people you are engaging with. Are they demonstrating introverted or extroverted behaviour? Based on your type, how does this affect the way you engage and how does it make you feel? Practise listening more and holding back if you're an extrovert, and if you are an introvert practise being more forthcoming and make more of an effort to give them more energy.

Choose someone you know who is the opposite type to you and spend at least five minutes with them today. Have a conversation to engage them to find out more about them. Make an effort to adapt to their needs using the ideas you had in the core exercise.

In your journal reflect on your day:

- What is still going around your head that you need to do more work on?
- What is squared away? What have you learnt?
- What three things will you do differently from now on?

- -

Week one, day three

On day three you will learn:

- what is positive about you
- how to win people over in the first seven seconds
- how to make quick positive connections.

Exercise: Week one, day thre
Your positive A to Z

- -

 It is just as important to be aware of your strengths and how to maximise them as it is to work on your weaknesses, so today's warm-up challenge is to find a positive adjective to describe you for every letter of the alphabet. They have to be true – don't just put in words to fill in the gaps.

Here is an example: A is for Appreciative of others; B is for Brave; and C is for Compassionate.

Using this to remind yourself how great and unique you are will help you with the rest of today's activities, which are about making positive first impressions.

 Let's say you have landed an interview for your dream job. How many seconds do you think it will take before the interviewers have decided if they like you, can trust you or would want to build a relationship with you?

Write your answer here:

Recent research gives the answer as between two and seven seconds – not even minutes. They make this snap judgment in seconds. First impressions are part of our survival mechanism as we decide quickly if we want someone in our lives. It is based on our flight and fight response.

The three most important questions people want answered in the first seconds are:

- Am I safe?

- Are you a winner or a loser?

- Are you worth letting into my world?

But don't panic – this is good news, not bad. If it only takes a few seconds to persuade someone you are worth talking to, it should be easy to boost these first few seconds of any meeting to ensure you get off to the perfect start.

The most important in a first impression are hands and eyes.

Ask people you trust for their feedback on your first impression. I asked my daughter and she told me that I came across as intimidating and aloof sometimes. I was shocked as that is not my intention at all, but my shyness in some more awkward situations was causing me to give that impression in my 'non-verbals'.

Analyse your non-verbals by giving yourself a mark out of ten for each of the following statements:

- I make strong eye contact and I don't look away too quickly.
- I never avoid a handshake (if this is possible).
- I always have my video on in virtual meetings if possible.
- My handshake is dry and firm.
- My hands are open.
- I use a lot of open gestures.
- I smile easily and naturally.

Top tip

Your posture conveys attitudes and feelings. Standing tall, pulling your shoulders back, and holding your head straight are signs of confidence and competence.

Connections start with eye contact. Today be aware of when you try to avoid eye contact and when you use your phone to avoid looking at people. Today make eye contact as much as possible and if it feels safe try an authentic smile.

To get you started try it in the following situations:

- As you get on public transport, with passengers and staff.
- When you buy your morning coffee.
- In the lift.
- Walking around your office.

Top tip

If this is hard for you, make it easier by giving yourself the task of identifying the eye colour of everyone you meet until it starts to feel more natural.

The perfect and safe way to try out your first impression and quick connections is by talking to working people, such as the coffee barista and staff at the supermarket checkout or petrol station. Avoid all forms of automation today and connect with eye contact, a smile and a brief conversation with as many working people as possible.

Virtual alternative – If you're working from home or won't have the opportunity to do this face to face, video meetings can give you a good workout. Remember eye contact is actually looking at the camera not at the person on the screen. This can be extremely difficult, so the best option is to alternate your eye contact from looking at the people on the screen and looking at the camera, particularly when you have something important to say.

Answer the following questions:

- How do you now feel about your first impression?
- What was most challenging for you?
- What worked and you can continue to use?

- -

Week one, day four

On day four you will learn how to:

- have a more positive outlook
- learn from role models
- develop your conversations.

Exercise: Week one, day four
Become a positive role model

- -

 We are all guilty of having negative thoughts or self-limiting beliefs but ask yourself what type of people you feel most drawn to? We are nearly always drawn to positive and optimistic people who make us feel good.

The Healthy Attitude Test (HAT) is a useful way to get a snapshot of how you are thinking, increase your self-awareness and make some quick changes.

If you are really happy with this area in your life and there is no room for improvement give yourself a 10, but if this part of your life is terrible give yourself a 1. And of course there is everything else in between. Fill in the pie chart below to see how you are doing.

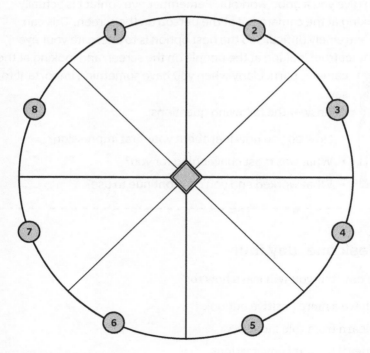

HAT pie chart

1 **Current position:** How is your life right now?

2 **What story are you telling others:** What are you telling other people about your life and your future?

3 **What story are you telling yourself:** What are you saying to yourself in your head?

4 **Appreciation:** Do you appreciate your achievements, however small, and how much are you appreciating the good things in your life?

5 **People you are connecting with:** Who are you mixing with? Do they make you feel good?

6 **What do you spend your time on:** Are you doing things that make you feel good?

7 **What do you want for the future:** What goals have you set yourself, if any?

8 **Your beliefs and expectations:** Do you believe they will happen?

On each of your lower scores, set yourself one goal that will take you in the right direction.

 Who is your role model? When it comes to engaging and connecting to people, my husband is my role model. We have been married nearly 30 years and I have learnt so much from him. He is able to connect with people easily anywhere because he is genuinely interested in people and he has the ability to make people feel good about themselves.

Who is your role model? Who do you know that has that X factor when it comes to connecting with people? In your journal answer the following questions about your chosen person:

• Why are they so successful and what do they specifically do that works?

• Write down six words that describe the way they connect.

• How would you describe them to other people?

Now that you have identified your role model, find time today to connect with them and ask for advice on how you can improve your ability to engage. Do this face to face if you can, but if not pick up the phone.

As an extra bonus asking for advice is a great way to engage, so don't be surprised if this relationship improves as well.

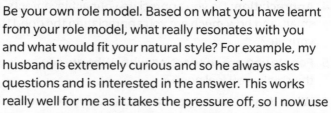

Be your own role model. Based on what you have learnt from your role model, what really resonates with you and what would fit your natural style? For example, my husband is extremely curious and so he always asks questions and is interested in the answer. This works really well for me as it takes the pressure off, so I now use this all of the time. Every opportunity you get today try different ways to spark a connection and see what works for you. To get you started:

- Make people laugh, keep it light.
- Give a genuine compliment.
- Change the questions 'How are you' to 'What's been the highlight of your day?'
- Listen for a hot topic to connect on.

Ask yourself some 'What' questions.

Recall a key moment from today and write down what happened and who was involved?

Take a few minutes to reflect and interpret the moment. What was the most important, interesting, relevant or useful aspect of the moment, idea or situation?

What you can learn from the moment and how it can be applied to you next time.

- -

Week one, day five

On day five you will learn:

- what makes a conversation deeper and more real
- how to SPARK up meaningful conversations.

Exercise: Week one, day five
More meaningful conversations

 Avoid conversation ruts. Most conversations go something like this: 'How are you?' or 'What do you do?' These are safe conversation starters, ritualistic ways to start a connection. There's nothing wrong with them but do you really care about the answers – probably not.

Next you pick up on something they say: 'I had a bad day, my boss keeps giving me more and more responsibility so I don't seem to have enough time in the day.'

Now it's your chance to talk about yourself: 'I know it's the same for me. I'm working on this crazy new client and they are so demanding.'

Back to them: 'Me too. I have this new client and they . . . '

The interaction becomes more and more competitive, driven by our need to talk about us. There is no judgment in this. It's an observation and if you don't believe me, go to a coffee shop for a few hours and listen to the conversations going on around you.

Think about conversations that weren't like this, where you found yourself feeling liked and appreciated and the other person was interested in you. Answer the following questions:

- What did they do that was different?
- How did it make you feel?
- How do you feel about them?

 To be interesting, be interested.

Dale Carnegie

If you are going to engage successfully with people and leave them with a lasting impression, SPARK up conversations instead.

SPARK stands for:

Safe questions to start to engage

Potential – don't listen so you can talk, but listen out for hot topics allowing them to do the talking

Ask curious follow-up questions on the potential hot subjects that come up

Reflect back your understanding and show your appreciation of them

Kind words – value what they have told you and say thank you

Here is a summary of how I used SPARK on my flight back from a holiday in Greece.

Holiday conversation

Me: How was your holiday?

Them: It was lovely and hot and a really beautiful place.

Me: What was the highlight for you?

Them: The weather, the food, snorkelling, but most of all being with the children. My life is very busy and it was great to have quality time with them.

Me: Was there anything in particular you did together that stuck out this time?

Them: We got a boat out and explored some lovely deserted coves, where we could snorkel and swim and then we had a picnic on the beach. It was a real adventure.

Me: Sounds like you have a great relationship with your kids, lots of fun.

Them: Yes, exactly we are really close.

Me: Lovely to talk to you, and thanks for the tip about the boat. We will definitely do that next time.

Think about a conversation you had very recently. How could you have changed that into a SPARK conversation?

A word of caution: This must be genuine – it's a powerful technique and if it's not real it's manipulation.

Pick someone you already have a good relationship with and find it easy to talk to (work or personal). Practise using SPARK with them. Afterwards reflect on how it felt and what was the response you got from them.

Top tip

Ask at least three questions about the potential in the conversation before you allow yourself to talk about yourself.

It's time to try this on someone you don't know well or a total stranger. Remember the three question rule: it's not that you can't talk about yourself as this can also build connection and rapport, but this way you help the other party feel liked and appreciated. As humans we like to reciprocate so the feeling will hopefully be mutual.

It's the end of the week, and one of the best ways to reflect is to take a short walk – reflection ramble. Take some time to think through your week. To get you started:

- What was the best thing that happened all week?
- Where did you add value or help someone?
- What have been your 'aha' moments and how will they change what you do in the future?

Progress check

Brilliant! You have made it through the first week and hopefully you're already seeing results and are motivated to get on with the next four weeks building your human skills. Today is an opportunity to review your progress and set goals for the next week, a bit like a weigh-in at the gym. Each week you will do the same three checks below.

Weekly reflection

I have been asking you to reflect all week in the warm-down sections, but now is the time to think more deeply about your week and answer the following questions in your journal honestly and openly:

- Did I do something that was out my comfort zone? How did it make me feel?
- What did I learn that would help me achieve my goals?
- How am I changing and what examples have I got that prove this?
- What can I do better or differently next week?
- What was the best thing that happened to me this week?
- What did I discover new about myself?
- What will I keep working on to improve myself?

Human roadmap

Go back to your human roadmap and review it carefully:

- Do you want to change anything?
- Have you stayed true to your personal values?

- Are you using your strengths?
- Are you developing the key areas you identified need working on, and what progress are you making?

SMARTER goals

SMART (Specific, Measurable, Achievable, Realistic and Time-bound) is great, but I have always felt there is something missing from this old favourite, so I have put my own spin on it. Let me explain.

I want to lose 6.5kg in six months, 1.5kg per month. This is realistic and fits with my lifestyle and I will weigh myself weekly to keep track of my progress. I am going to do this by eating healthy food, not drinking alcohol during the week and going to the gym three times a week.

My goal is SMART but it's a bit uninspiring and dull because what is missing is the heart and spirit of the goal. We need to make it SMARTER:

- Excite – Emotion
- Result – Why you are doing it

I want to lose weight because I am going to my sister's wedding in six month's time in South Africa. We are really close and I am so excited for her and as I am running the ceremony I want to look my absolute best in a beautiful dress.

When you set a SMARTER goal you connect with the emotions and the reason you want to achieve it. This will really motivate you. Go to your journal and set a SMARTER goal for next week. It can be something related to the Week one Engage that you want to carry on working on, or it can be related to Week two Listen. We will review this goal in next week's progress check.

chapter 6

Week two: Listen

Slowing down and asking questions from a place of curiosity, listening to understand rather than to respond

There's a huge difference between hearing and listening: hearing is part of our survival instincts as we are programmed to react to a sound. We take a full second to respond to something we notice out of the corner of our eye, but react ten times quicker to a sound. It's our first alarm system. You'll have seen herds of animals react in a split second to a sound, especially if there is a predator. And we are no different, meaning that hearing is an automatic response and active listening is a conscious skill, which demands more focus and energy than just about anything else.

Hearing	Listening
Unintentional	Intentional
Automatic	Voluntary
Easy	Difficult

As listening is one of the best ways to engage and build meaningful relationships with others, I will be revisiting one of the key models covered last week – SPARK. This is because listening is critical to ensuring SPARK is used in an authentic and powerful way. This week the focus is on understanding your own personal barriers to being in the moment and listening, as well as how to be conscious and active.

Before we start, conscious listening is exhausting so give your gift wisely and don't do too much in one day.

Week two, day one

On day one you will learn:

- why great listening changes the way people see you

- what makes someone a great listener
- how to identify your own barriers to listening, taking you out of the moment.

Exercise: Week two, day one
Brilliant listening

- -

 Answer the following questions honestly in your journal. Which of these three statements is closest to the way you are thinking and feeling?:

- I am already a good listener and I could probably skip this week.
- I think listening is a natural ability – some people are just better listeners than others.
- I know I need to improve my listening and I am really looking forward to this week to find out about some useful tools and techniques to help me.

If your answer is a), it's good to recognise your strengths. When you are working out at the gym, even if your legs or biceps are strong you still need to work on them to keep them in tip-top shape. As listening is a conscious active skill it needs work to maintain it.

If your answer is b), hearing is definitely natural while listening isn't. It's a learnt human skill that takes a lot of commitment, hard work and practice and that's great news for all of us because we can all learn to be good listeners.

If your answer is c), that's a good answer and shows a healthy mindset. I think you will enjoy this week as the exercises are fun, powerful and life-changing, not just at work but in your personal relationships too.

 Think of three people from any part of your life who you consider to be brilliant listeners.

Write their names down in your journal. For each person give them a tick for some or all of the following:

- I like them.
- I love them.
- I respect them.

If you are anything like me each person will have at least two ticks. This is because we are attracted to people who are interested in us. In Week one we worked on how using SPARK helps engage and connect and it relies on us being curious about other people's stories. Being a great listener is one of the best ways to be liked, loved and respected and really stand out. It's funny that listening is often underrated but a great listener is admired and never forgotten.

In your journal write down three things that are common to all three of your great listeners. To get you started consider the following:

- They ask questions.
- They give me eye contact.
- They ask follow-up questions.
- They are present and in the moment.

Three minutes of silence every day has been proven to help with our overall awareness and mindfulness, which in turn helps us to be more effective listeners. Starting today and then every day this week find three minutes to be totally silent and aware of everything going on around you. To get you started:

- Focus on your breathing.
- What can you hear (birdsong, traffic, air conditioning)?
- How do you feel (warm, cold, hungry, thirsty)?

Remember SPARK from the end of Week one? Have at least one conversation today with someone and be more aware of your listening. Think about the following:

- What stops you listening and makes it more challenging?
- Are you listening to respond or are you able to park your agenda?
- What takes you out of the moment? Are you thinking about something else and what is it?

Top tip

Listening takes a tremendous amount of energy and effort, which makes it very tiring, so be gentle on yourself, you are human after all.

 Based on the exercises today, what were your main barriers to listening? It's extremely important to identify and be aware of these because they stop you being in the moment and present, both essential for conscious listening. So you can work on them; write them down in your journal. To get you started consider the following:

- Distractions – noise, chatter, phones.
- Flare-ups – are you thinking about what they have said or making associations?
- Wandering mind – are you thinking about random things?
- Mental rehearsal – are you thinking ahead, problem-solving or waiting to speak?

Week two, day two

On day two you will learn how:

- different communication styles impact on your listening
- listening isn't just using your ears
- to engage more of your senses when listening.

Exercise: Week two, day two
Listening with your senses

- -

 This is your second chance to understand more about your personality type and appreciate other people's differences. This week it's linked to listening.

What are your strengths and challenges as a conscious listener? Consider the statements below. It may depend on who you are with or the environment, but where are you most comfortable?

Statement one: I am more distracted by my need to speak rather than my need to think.

If you are distracted by your own need to speak, this is another indication of extroverted behaviour. If on the other hand, you need to think, this is another indication of introverted behaviour.

Extroverts give introverts more space to answer your questions. Don't be tempted to clip them and answer for them.
Introverts give extroverts more feedback showing interest. In other words, you're listening with verbal nods and body language but it has to be genuine.

Statement two: I am more likely to hear and take in facts and figures than emotions and feelings.

If you hear facts and figures more easily you are more likely to be a thinker coming from the head first. If you hear emotions and feelings you are more likely to be a feeler coming from the heart first.

As a **thinker**, you pick up key facts and the logical side of a conversation. Work on paying more attention to the message behind the words and the emotions, especially if you are talking to a feeler type.

As a **feeler**, you pick up the message behind the words and the emotions, but may miss the key facts or find yourself making assumptions. Ask more questions to understand the facts.

Statement three: I find it hard to listen to lots of detail without knowing the bigger picture.

You are more likely to be a big picture type, making it hard for you to hear or even be interested in the detail if you don't know the reason behind it. On the other hand, you may be a detailed and practical type, wanting to know all the information.

Detailed types ask questions to get the detail you need, rather than being frustrated by the information being vague.
Big picture types tell the other party you need to know where the detail is going first so you can concentrate, or ask what the context is.

 To listen effectively, we need to engage all our senses in the right way, but each area can throw up challenges.

In the table below, write your ideas in the solution box on what you can do to use your senses in the right way. I have given you one for each to get you started.

What we listen with	Challenges	Solutions
Ears – the hardware	Hearing is not listening as it is more about our survival; listening is more conscious	1. Make a commitment to slow down and listen 2. 3.

What we listen with	Challenges	Solutions
Eyes	Noticing non-verbals is good but we can make assumptions or read them wrongly	1. Be more aware of all of the non-verbals, eyes, body and vocal tone 2. 3.
Brains	We all have our own values, beliefs, memories and associations, so we may hear what we want to hear	1. Ask questions to clarify 2. 3.
Gut	We have as many brain neurons in our gut as a cat's brain, leading us to make snap judgments	1. Be aware of the judgments you are making and test them with questions as you might be wrong 2. 3.

Do your three minutes of mindful silence and then put on a piece of music. Try and focus on the music itself – can you pick out all the instruments. If your mind wanders (which it will), make a mental note of what you think about and then refocus.

Top tip

Use a closed question to test your assumptions: Would you prefer it if I did the presentation today? Have I worried you?

In your listening today, practise engaging all of the senses. Be more aware of the non-verbals and the space you are listening in. What is your gut telling you and is your brain leaping to assumptions. Use the ideas that you came up with in the core exercise to be more in the moment and listen more effectively. To get you started:

- Test assumptions by asking questions.
- Reflect back your understanding of what they have said: 'It sounds like you had a challenging meeting, but you're happy with how it went.'
- Be patient and listen to the end before making judgments.

In your journal answer the following questions

- How did you find engaging with more than one of the senses when listening?
- What impact did it have on your listening?
- What one thing will you do differently from now on?

- -

Week two, day three

On day three you will learn:

- what is active listening and the benefits
- different types of questions and how to use them
- how to improve the A of SPARK.

Exercise: Week two, day three
Active listening

- -

Yesterday we looked at how being more aware of everything going on around you is vital to good listening, and that hearing is very different from active listening. The table below shows the benefits of active listening. As a bonus, being active is the best way to slow yourself down to be more conscious, focused and in the moment.

Give yourself a mark out of 10 for how you use each of them.
 What can you do to improve each of the scores?

Active listening	Benefits	Score out of 10	Ways to improve
Active silence	Speaker can think and express their feelings Listener can reflect on what has been said (or not said)		
Asking questions	Speaker is able to answer questions that allow them to expand on their thoughts, ideas or story Listener is able to clarify and test their assumptions		
Reflecting	Acknowledges the speaker's feelings Checks the accuracy of the listening of the said and unsaid		
Summarising	Communicates the listener's understanding to the speaker Describes the listener's understanding in their own words		

 Why ask questions? A key part of active listening is being able to ask effective questions. This isn't just a nice skill to have, it's actually a survival skill in work or business situations, not to mention its importance in successful personal relationships. Questions allow you to check your understanding of complicated briefs, deal with conflict, facilitate meetings, solve problems, coach, interview – and that's only scratching the surface.

Types of key questions

Open questions: elicit full answers When, what, how, who, where, why What are your thoughts on my proposal? How will you improve your performance?	**Closed questions**: elicit yes or no answers) Do, can, will, are, have, shall Do you like my proposal? Can you can make improvements?
Commands: not strictly speaking questions, but still gather information Tell me about, explain, give me an example, talk me through Talk me through your ideas for my proposal? Tell me how you can improve your performance?	**Follow-up questions**: signal you are interested and often when we get the real information and insights For instance? Such as? Tell me more?

Linear questioning or QAQAQAQA

Linear probing is where the question gives us an answer and then this becomes the mother or father of the next question. Linear questioning is a powerful way to stay on the speaker's agenda and really dig down to get a deeper understanding. It's an essential skill for salespeople, leaders, customer service and anyone who wants to solve problems and understand people's needs.

Here is an example.
'The course you're on, how are you finding it?
'It's challenging if I'm honest.'
'Really, why?'
'I think it's because it's really experiential and I am having to go outside of my comfort zone.'
'How do you feel about that?'

'As I said it's challenging, but I like being challenged and I am really enjoying it.'

Can you see how it would have been easy to have jumped in with assumptions when they said it was challenging, yet one more question gave us the full story.

Top tip

Avoid leading questions: 'Don't you think you should put more examples in your proposal?' Or 'Do you think you should put more work into your proposal?' These are questions you already know the answer to because it's your agenda.

Do your three minutes of silence exercise.

Be the interviewer. Pick someone at work you know less well or a family member or friend (the great thing about listening is you can practise any time) By using a variety of different question types, including QAQA-QAQA, find out something that you don't already know about them. In this exercise resist the temptation to talk about yourself – give them five to ten minutes of quality curiosity.

Here are some questions to get you started:

- What was the highlight of your day?
- What exciting things have you got going on in your life right now?
- Tell me what are you working on right now?
- What are you up to this weekend?

This is another chance to practise your SPARK conversations. I want you to choose someone you know really well and you can trust to give you feedback (don't tell them in advance though). During the conversation focus on asking curious questions using the QAQAQAQA technique to help the speaker tell their story. Experiment with the different types of questions and make some mental notes on what worked and opened them up and any that didn't.

Afterwards ask them for some feedback:

- How did they feel?
- What feedback do they have on your listening?
- What would help you move forward?

Remember this exercise? In your journal reflect on your day:

- What is still going around your head that you need to do more work on?
- What is squared away? What have you learnt?
- What three things will you do differently from now on?

- -

Week two, day four

On day four you will learn how to:

- identify your inner critic and reframe your thinking
- develop active silence through simple meditation
- learn from your great listeners.

Exercise: Week two, day four
Learn from the experts

- -

You are going to discover how to reframe your negative thoughts into positive learning experiences. In your journal carry out the task below.

Think of a conversation where you were preoccupied or came away not clear on what the other person said: Then consider these questions:

- What did you do that didn't help you?
- Why did you do these things?
- What, if anything, was the impact on the other person or situation?

If you found it easy to be hard on yourself, your inner critic is speaking and it is often harsher than anyone else. We can then start to focus on this and it starts to be part of our belief system. For example, 'I'm a terrible listener, I'm just selfish and talk all the time.' The best way to silence the inner critic is to pull out the positives and reframe your negative thoughts into opportunities to learn.

In the conversation where you didn't listen effectively:

- What were the positives that came out of it?
- What did you learn from the situation?
- How has this changed the way you do things now or how could it change the way you do things in the future?

 **Silent and listen are spelt with the same letters – think about that.**

Alfred Brendel

Yesterday we looked at active listening and how the silence you leave allows you to hear the other person's thoughts instead of your own, without experiencing the conversation through your own lens.

As part of the sprint exercises this week I have been asking you to do three minutes of silence every day to practise being quiet. Today we are going to take this one stage further and do a short meditation exercise for just ten minutes. Meditation is a great way to develop calmness, slow down your busy mind and is brilliant for stress.

Follow the instructions below and enjoy:

1 Sit comfortably and quietly with your eyes closed and effortlessly and silently inside repeat a word or a short phrase. This can be anything you like. For example, it could be calm, peace, silence, listen or you could combine the words to make a short phrase. I use 'calm, peace and silence' as I find saying this over and over again calms my mind and gives me focus.

2 Then continue to sit quietly with your eyes closed and do nothing for one minute. During that time thoughts will come, notice those thoughts come without any effort. After a minute or so, start thinking your word or phrase in the same effortless way as the thoughts came during the minute.

3 Slowly in your head repeat your word or phrase in that same effortless way for about eight minutes. Thoughts will come and that's ok. Having thoughts during meditation is natural. When they do come gently return to thinking your word in the same effortless way.

Top tip

Don't try to meditate or make anything happen. When you 'try to make meditation happen' it can cause pressure in your head or even give you a headache. The key to meditating is to do nothing.

Early on this week you identified three great listeners. Now connect with as many of them as you can and ask them for advice on how to improve your listening skills. To get you started, ask:

- What are your top tips to be a better listener?
- How do you stay focused and in the moment?
- How do I stop myself interrupting and taking over?
- When I find myself drifting off how can I stop myself?

Take what you have learnt from your great listeners. Decide what really resonates with you and what would fit your natural style. For example, one of my great listeners is an actor I work with in my training business. He has the most amazing calm and patient manner and he asks thoughtful questions and never interrupts me when I answer. This inspires me because I love to talk and it's something I am working on all the time. Every opportunity you get today, try out the advice you have been given.

Recall a key moment from today and write down what happened and who was involved.

Take a few minutes to reflect and interpret the moment. What was the most important, interesting, relevant or useful aspect of the moment, idea or situation?

Then reflect on what you can learn from the moment and how it can be applied to you next time.

Week two, day five

On day five you will learn:

- what type of listener you are
- how to SPARK up meaningful conversations.

Exercise: Week two, day five
Your listening type

Practise your meditation again today.

Now you have a much clearer understanding of what conscious active listening entails, and you have been made fully aware of your own listening all week, I want you to be brutally honest and evaluate yourself below.

Rate yourself 1 to 5 on the scale of 1 being 'no way' and 5 being 'yes that's me'. My highest scores make me a 'butt in' and a 'problem-solver'. When you find out yours make some comments and action points to help you improve.

Listening type	Rating	Comments and action points
The pretender – nod, make eye contact but your mind is somewhere else	1 2 3 4 5	
The butt in – find it hard to allow the speaker to finish and signal you are anxious to speak	1 2 3 4 5	
The assessor – find yourself judging the speaker, connect to content from your own framework and find it hard to feel empathy	1 2 3 4 5	
The hanger – use the speaker's words to activate your own memories and associations, allowing you to speak about things that are often unrelated	1 2 3 4 5	
The disapprover – listen mainly to find points to debate and disagree with	1 2 3 4 5	
The problem-solver – your goal is to give advice and solve problems	1 2 3 4 5	

 Spend the whole day without interrupting. Just resist the urge to jump in. Sit and listen, even if it is past your normal tolerance level. This doesn't mean you can't talk – you are just not going to interrupt. Be aware how hard this is and what you would have interrupted for.

Your final challenge this week is to use everything you have learnt to engage and listen to at least one complete stranger. You need to be open to the opportunity to connect first of all (when you get on the train, bus, go into a coffee shop or walk your dog,). Instead of avoiding strangers, stop and say hello. Your mission is to consciously listen and let go of any personal agenda, judgments and biases. I did this every day for 30 days as an experiment and it was eye-opening. I made some amazing connections and met some fascinating people.

If you are thinking that people will be resistant, you are right. There is that possibility, but out of the people I listened to only a few didn't want to engage with me. Sometimes it took a few minutes for it to become comfortable and you will know when to give up. But ask questions, be active, use silence, engage your senses and commit totally to it and you may be very pleasantly surprised.

Top tip

When you listen, physically let go and relax your body, give yourself permission to not talk about you or solve their problem. It's ok to be simply curious.

It's the end of the week and one of the best ways to reflect is to take a short walk – your reflection ramble. Take some time to think through your week. To get you started ask yourself:

- What was the best thing that happened all week?

- Where did you add value or help someone?

- What have been your 'aha' moments and how will they change what you do in the future?

Progress check

Week two is done so it's time to check in on your progress and set goals for next week.

Weekly reflection

Answer the following questions in your journal honestly and openly.

- Did I do something that was out of my comfort zone? How did it make me feel?
- What did I learn that would help me achieve my goals?
- How am I changing and what examples have I got that prove this?
- What can I do better or differently next week?
- What was the best thing that happened to me this week?
- What did I discover new about myself?
- What will I keep working on to improve myself?

Human roadmap

Go back to your human roadmap and review it carefully:

- Do you want to change anything?
- Have you stayed true to your personal values?
- Are you using your strengths?
- Are you developing the key areas you identified need working on, and what progress are you making?

SMARTER goals

You set a SMARTER goal at the end of last week. Now review how you did by answering the following questions in your journal:

- Was this goal easier or harder than expected?
- Overall, are you happy with your progress? If you are, then great! If not, work out why and fix the problem.
- What are you doing well towards this goal? And keep doing it.
- What do you need to do better to achieve this goal? And do better.
- Are you enjoying this goal, or at least excited about the end result? Reward yourself for achieving mini-goals and milestones to keep you on your journey. Remember, the end result needs to be something you really want.

Top tip

Remember that conscious human skills are never finished. They need constant commitment so don't worry if you need to keep working on your goal and remember the 'not yet' rule.

In your journal set another SMARTER goal for next week. It can be something related to the Engage or Listen weeks that you want to carry on working on or it can be related to Week 3 Empathise. We will review this goal in next week's progress check.

chapter 7

Week three:
Empathise

A genuine desire to understand someone else's experience

> **The action of understanding, being aware of, being sensitive to, and vicariously experiencing the feelings, thoughts, and experience of another.**
>
> *Merriam Webster Dictionary*

To feel and display empathy, it is not necessary to share the same experiences or circumstances as others. Rather, empathy is an attempt to better understand the other person by getting to know their perspective.

Neuroscientists have recently discovered that humans are wired to experience empathy through multiple systems of mirror neurons in our brains. These mirror neurons are the primary physiological basis of emotional empathy. However, it's a little more complicated than that. You learnt in the last chapter that hearing is natural and listening is learnt. Empathy is similar as emotional empathy is more natural while compassionate empathy once again is more conscious and needs to be developed.

Psychologists Daniel Goleman and Paul Ekman identified three different types of empathy.

Type of empathy	Example	Comment	Downsides
Cognitive therapy	A doctor will want to help a sick patient by understanding the illness rather than involving themselves in it.	The ability to know how a person feels and what they are thinking. It responds to a problem with intellect.	Can be disconnected from or ignore deep emotions. It doesn't put you in another's shoes in a felt sense.
Emotional empathy	Crying at a wedding or cringing when someone stubs their toe. It's a gut reaction that often feels like an instinctive human response.	The ability to share the feelings of another person. This type of empathy helps you build emotional connections with others.	Can be overwhelming or inappropriate in certain circumstances.

Type of empathy	Example	Comment	Downsides
Compassionate empathy	Someone comes to you in tears and you want to understand why they are upset and you share in their emotional experience by listening and offering help and support.	Also known as empathic concern. This goes beyond simply understanding others and sharing their feelings. It actually moves you to take action, to help however you can.	Few, as this is the type of empathy that we should be striving for.

Week three, day one

On day one you will learn:

• how lack of empathy impacts on you

• how to empathise with yourself

• good and bad practice from observing others.

Exercise: Week three, day one
Understanding empathy

- -

Answer the following question honestly in your journal.

Which of these four statements is closest to the way you are thinking and feeling?

(a) I am worried that empathy can come across as insincere and fake.

(b) Empathising comes naturally to me and I find it easy.

(c) I am curious to understand more about empathy and how I can use it in an authentic way.

(d) I don't really understand what empathy is or why it's important in the workplace.

If your answer is a), I understand this response as some people use empathy in the wrong way and it can be passive aggressive or insincere. Phrases like 'I understand how you feel' or 'I appreciate your concerns' can sound glib and disingenuous. In this chapter the focus is on being authentic and seeking to understanding how people feel rather than just saying it.

If your answer is b), that's good to hear and as humans we are all naturally wired to emotional empathy, but we still need to develop our skills in compassionate empathy. Use the masterclass to build on your natural abilities and be more aware.

If your answer is c), that's a great answer and shows a healthy mindset. Stay curious throughout this week and you won't go too far wrong.

If your answer is d), that's a very honest answer and you will be surprised by how many people probably feel the same. To give you a business case for empathy the Global Empathy Index reports that the top ten companies generated 50% more earnings than the bottom ten.

 I was working flat out, travelling to the US and then to Australia. I was running training courses most days and I think I was getting close to burnout. All I needed from my family was some empathy. Just some questions like 'How are you doing?, 'Where are you struggling?' or 'How can we help and support you?'

Instead, the resentment I was feeling around being taken for granted exploded in a full-on family argument, leaving me exhausted and feeling guilty.

Think of a time when you needed empathy yourself and it didn't happen or it was done badly. Answer the questions below in your journal and be really honest in your answers:

• What was happening to you? Describe the situation.

• What were you feeling? Describe your emotions.

- What did the people around you do?
- What was missing? Describe the empathetic behaviours that would have helped you.

To be empathetic with others, you first need to learn to do it for yourself and be more in tune with your own feelings.

Set three alarms during the course of the day (you can time them for your normal breaks so you have time to reflect). When the alarm goes off, ask yourself how you are feeling and what is your current mood. Be really aware of your emotions. To get you started, here are some feelings:

- I feel tired.
- I feel bored.
- I feel energised and motivated.
- I feel worried and nervous.

Do this every day this week to train yourself to be more conscious of your feelings and emotions and this will help you to empathise more with other people.

When you are in a public place or even at home today discreetly listen in on someone else's conversation – some polite eavesdropping. Listen for the following:

- the emotions involved
- the perspective of each person
- how well the people communicated (did they appear to be listening, did they talk over each other, were they distracted).

Also be aware of their body language.

Listening to others can help you be more aware and help you to recognise good and bad practice.

Top tip

Observing others in social situations or when you're a customer really helps to identify good and bad practice.

Now you have more of an understanding around your own needs and emotions, it will help you to apply them to others. So, I want you to come full circle from the warm-up where you thought about your own situation and think of a time when someone you know needed empathy from you and you know that what you did at the time was lacking.

What would you do differently if you could go back in time and get a second chance?

Week three, day two

On day two you will learn:

- whether you are more a thinker or a feeler
- the benefits of each type of empathy
- how to use empathetic questions.

Exercise: Week three, day two
Practise empathy

- -

This week the self-awareness exercise focuses on whether you come from your head or your heart when you are making judgments or decisions. This can impact on the type of empathy you find easier to give.

Are you a thinker or a feeler? There is no judgment in your answers to the questions below. If you come out as a thinker that does not mean you are cold-hearted and unfeeling. And if you are more the feeler type that doesn't mean you wear fluffy bunny ears and cry at every sad film.

1 What is more important to you?
  (a) Compassion
  (b) Fair judgment

2 What is your natural reaction when a friend tells you about a relationship problem?

   (a) I will listen very carefully so I can understand and connect with the person

   (b) I will help the person find a solution

3 What is the best way to persuade you?

   (a) Strong emotional appeal

   (b) A great logical explanation

4 How would you describe yourself as leading?

   (a) From the heart

   (b) From the head

Mostly a): You have a leaning towards a feeling preference.

Mostly b): You have a leaning towards a thinking preference.

Thinkers	Feelers
Search for logical explanations or solutions	Are very sensitive to conflict
Value fairness above all else	Make decisions based on relationships
Believe the truth is more important than being tactful	React with strong feelings to interpersonal challenges
Want to solve problems	Want to create harmony

Thinkers and feelers are likely to experience empathy differently. Feelers are more likely to connect emotionally and thinkers cognitively.

 At the beginning of this chapter I introduced you to the three types of empathy (cognitive, emotional and compassionate). In your journal note down an example of each type of empathy that you have experienced yourself. Then consider these questions:

• What was your response to each of these?

• Were they helpful and appropriate to you at the time?

• What is the benefit of each type?

Choose a person you are having relationship difficulties with – it doesn't have to be major. It could be one of the people you identified earlier in the book as being a less warm (cool) relationship.

- **Stage one:** Do they see things differently from you? Step into their shoes. For example, imagine doing their job and the challenges and issues they face.

- **Stage two:** Think about the conversations you have had with that person. Consciously, check your interpretations of what they said and consider what questions you could have asked to understand more about their perspective.

Listening and empathy are the perfect partners because we can't always share people's feelings but we can always seek to understand their feelings. The questions and reflective statements below deepen your listening skills. A person who sees a listener as really trying to understand their meaning will be willing to explore their problems and their self more deeply.

Questions:

1 Help me understand, tell me how are you are feeling?

2 What impact is this having on you?

3 What do you need right now?

4 How can I help you?

Reflective statements:

1 It sounds like you have strong feelings on this.

2 I can see how important this is to you.

3 I understand why you feel this way.

4 I know how you feel.

Think of someone you are comfortable with who needs an empathetic ear today and give them a call. In a genuine way try out some of the questions and statements as and when they are appropriate.

Top tip

Rather than saying 'I understand' say 'I want to understand'. This is powerful because it's not making any assumptions and suggests you care enough to listen.

In your journal answer the following questions:

- What did you like most about today's activities, and why?
- What surprised you today and why?
- What did you learn from today's activities?

- -

Week three, day three

On day three you will learn:

- the difference between empathy and sympathy
- the benefits of being transported by stories
- how changing your perspective increases your empathy.

Exercise: Week three, day three
Empathy and sympathy

- -

Empathising is also sometimes mistaken for sympathising, but they are very different responses. Sympathy is primarily about observation and an acceptance that someone else is going through challenging experiences. It can amount to feeling sorry for someone, which is an acknowledgment of a situation. It's not a concept that requires someone to experience the emotion that another person is going through deeply. Sympathy is 'feeling with' instead of deeply feeling for them. With this, there's a natural detachment from the situation.

The critical difference between empathy and sympathy is that instead of feeling with someone, you're feeling for them. You're experiencing a fraction of their emotions and feelings because you see things from their perspective.

Empathise	Sympathise
Personal	General
Seeking to understand	Feeling pity
Understanding	Caring
Positive and negative situations	Negative situations
Feeling it with them	Acknowledging it about them
Shared	Expressed

Think about a time when you showed sympathy. What did you say and do?

Then think about a time when you showed empathy. What did you say and do?

 Telling your story is an important part of being human but if you want to work on your empathy skills you need to be a story hearer as well.

When people hear a compelling empathy-evoking story, their brain creates oxytocin. But we also know that for a story to motivate action it must do more than evoke empathy – it must also capture and hold our attention, transporting us into the world of the character.

What stories create this sort of reaction in you? Brainstorm in your journal the books you've read, the films you've watched, the TV or videos that make you feel something.

Over the rest of this week choose to watch or read stories that transport you and make you feel. These will give your empathy muscle a workout. So enjoy.

Find ways to get out of your usual environment. The more you experience different things, the more you can develop your empathic responses. So, do something different today that changes your environment and perspective. It will give you a better appreciation of others. To get you started:

- Take a different transport, walk or go a different way to work.
- Instead of emailing a colleague, speak to them.
- Stop and talk to a homeless person.
- Go somewhere different for lunch or coffee.
- If you are in a meeting sit next to someone you know less well.

 We all have biases and judgments – even something silly like I prefer dogs to cats and I relate better to dog people than cat people. Highly empathetic people challenge their own preconceptions and prejudices by searching for what they share with people rather than what divides them.

Choose someone who is very different from you at work – maybe they are younger or older, from a different country or background or do a very different job. Have a coffee with them or stop by and start a conversation. Use SPARK to create a connection and ask curious questions to find out more about them. Look for where you can connect and find out their story. Really listen to them and where you find a connection open up and share your thoughts and feelings. Tell your story.

Virtual option – If you are having video meetings with colleagues or customers spend a little bit of time at the beginning to find out more about them.

Top tip

Don't be disheartened if people don't make the same effort to listen to you. You can only work on yourself.

 In your journal use the following questions to reflect on your day:

- What is still going around your head that you need to do more work on?

- What is squared away? What have you learnt?
- What three things will you do differently from now on?

- -

Week three, day four

On day four you will learn:

- how to get unstuck when facing challenges
- how to understand body language
- what empathy feels like and how you can learn from it.

Exercise: Week three, day four
Reading between the lines

- -

 How are you doing? We are about halfway through the masterclass and I am sure there have been challenges along the way. Today I am going to give you a way to help you get unstuck when you are facing difficulties in anything at work or in your personal life.

One of the main reasons we get stuck is we spend too much time thinking *why* has this happened to us. We spend so much time asking 'Why?' questions it can make us seem powerless.

To get out of this 'stuck' mode of thinking, start asking 'What' questions and then, ask 'How' questions. That should lead to a course of action that will change your situation.

An excessive use of 'why-based' questions focuses on justification, judgment, blame and excessive analysis. In this respect they don't actually create *movement*. 'What-based' and 'how-based' questions encourage us to search for solutions in moving us forward with movement and action. Here are some examples:

Why am I such a failure?
What can I learn from this experience?
How can I act differently next time so that I get a better result?

Why can't it just be easy?
What do I need to make it easier?
How can I do it?

Why did I say that?
What effect did my words have?
How can I phrase it next time so that I get the results I want?

What are you stuck on right now? It can be anything. Try the Why? What? How? technique and see where it takes you.

 Empathy is at the heart of an actor's art.

Meryl Streep

I use actors in my behavioural training courses because they are trained in reading between the lines and are able to demonstrate the subtle nuances of body language. In the Listen week we looked at how listening with our eyes is important if we want to understand the full picture. Observing and reacting to body language, vocal tone or energy is even more important if you want to be more empathetic.

These are some comfort signals:

- Leaning in, moving closer, or turning to face you

- Good even eye contact

- Open gestures

- Smiling

And these are some discomfort signals:

- Turned away or feet turning away

- Moving back or turning away

- No or little eye contact

- Neck touching or rubbing

To practise being more aware of body language, watch a reality TV programme (there are plenty to choose from) and have a notepad and pen ready. Note when you see any of the signs of comfort or discomfort. If you want to really test yourself, watch another programme with the TV muted and see if you can still pick up the signs.

You are now going to do some people watching. It's time to take your observations into real life and observe interactions with people as you go about your day. Watch for the body language between two or more people. Then test yourself by asking yourself the following questions:

- What am I reading between the lines?
- What emotions am I seeing?
- Is the body language comfortable or uncomfortable?

For this exercise you need someone you are close to and can totally trust so you can ask them to give you feedback on your ability to be empathetic. Pick someone you have shown empathy for in the past six months and ask them for specific feedback on the following:

- How empathetic was I?
- How was my non-verbal communication?
- How did I make you feel?
- What if anything could I do differently?

Recall a key moment from today and write down what happened and who was involved.

Take a few minutes to reflect and interpret the moment. What was the most important, interesting, relevant or useful aspect of the moment, idea or situation?

What can you learn from the moment and how can it be applied to you next time?

Week three, day five

On day five you will learn how:

- you now see empathy and why
- to use your role model's advice
- to use GROW to map out an empathetic conversation.

Exercise: Week three, day five
You and empathy

- -

 At the end of this week how are you now viewing empathy? Read the inspirational quotes below and see what speaks to you and is aligned with your thinking (there is no right or wrong answer). Pick one of them that resonates with you, copy it into your journal and then note down next to it why it speaks to you.

'Empathy is seeing with the eyes of another, listening with the ears of another, and feeling with the heart of another.' **Anonymous**

'Empathy is about finding echoes of another person in yourself.' **Mohsin Hami**

'We think we listen, but very rarely do we listen with real understanding, true empathy. Yet listening, of this very special kind, is one of the most potent forces for change that I know.' **Carl Rogers**

'Be kind, for everyone you meet is fighting a hard battle.' **Plato**

'Empathy takes time, and efficiency is for things, not people.' **Stephen Covey**

 GROW (Goals, Reality, Options, Way Forward) is a fantastic coaching model that I use in my work to help people understand and reach their goals. But it can also be used for self-coaching, which is how you are going to use it today to help you work on an important relationship.

Choose a person or a relationship you know needs some TLC (it can be work or personal). Below are two GROW templates: A is an example to help you and B is for you to work on.

Top tip

Choose someone you are comfortable with and will be easy to see today (mine was my daughter). They don't have to be going through anything difficult as this is about giving them some time.

My Goal	Their Reality	My Goal	Their Reality
To help her feel valued Let her know I care	Difficult job Missing her partner Money worries Doubts and fears about her future		

Options	Way Forward	Options	Way Forward
Cup of coffee just the two of us Ask her how she's doing Tell her how amazing she is Offer her support with money	Send her a text right now Ask her when she's free Take a little gift to cheer her up		

GROW example and template

You are now going to learn from a role model. This is the regular weekly spot to learn from someone you see as a role model, who has been empathetic and compassionate to you. In your journal answer the following questions:

- How do they show you empathy?
- How do they make you feel?
- What can you learn from them?

Meet them, phone them, email them or message them asking for advice on the GROW plan you completed in the warm-up.

Put GROW into action. This definitely needs to be done face to face, so set an appropriate time and place to meet with your chosen person and have your compassionate empathetic conversation.

Afterwards reflect on how it went, and specifically, if they reacted differently to you.

It's the end of the week and it's time for a walk to take some time to think through your week – your reflection ramble. To get you started ask yourself these questions:

- What was the best thing that happened all week?
- Where did you add value or help someone?
- What have been your 'aha' moments and how will they change what you do in the future?

- -

Progress check

Week three is done and it's time to check in on your progress and set goals for next week.

Weekly reflection

Answer the following questions in your journal honestly and openly.

- Did I do something that was out of my comfort zone? How did it make me feel?
- What did I learn that would help me achieve my goals?
- How am I changing and what examples have I got that prove this?
- What can I do better or differently next week?
- What was the best thing that happened to me this week?
- What did I discover new about myself?
- What will I keep working on to improve myself?

Human roadmap

Go back to your human roadmap and review it carefully:

- Do you want to change anything?
- Have you stayed true to your personal values?
- Are you using your strengths?
- Are you developing the key areas you identified need working on, and what progress are you making?

SMARTER goals

You set a SMARTER goal at the end of last week. Now review how you did by answering the following questions in your journal:

- Was this goal easier or harder than expected?
- Overall, are you happy with your progress? If you are, then great! If not, work out why and fix the problem.
- What are you doing well towards this goal? And keep doing it!
- What do you need to do better to achieve this goal? And do it better!
- Are you enjoying this goal, or at least excited about the end result? Reward yourself for achieving mini-goals and milestones to keep you on your journey. Remember, the end result needs to be something you really want.

Top tip

You can go back and repeat exercises if you enjoyed them. This is not just a five-week masterclass – it's for life.

In your journal set another SMARTER goal for next week. It can be something related to the previous weeks that you want to carry on working on or it can be related to Week five Inspire. We will review this goal in next week's progress check.

chapter 8

Week four:
Collaborate

**Build, manage and collaborate in the
teams of the future**

The first thing to say about this chapter is we are talking about the human side of collaboration and not the technical or software side. There are some amazing tools out there to help already effective teams collaborate (especially remotely), but collaboration is as much about people's interaction with each other as about the tools we use.

Don't forget the previous three chapters have built skills essential for teamwork and collaboration. So we will be revisiting some of the exercises but this time with more of a focus on working together in and across teams.

This is the definition we are going to work with as collaboration is a big subject. This helps keep things simple and practical.

Two or more people working together towards shared goals.

This simple definition includes three parts:

- Two or more people (team)
- Working together (processes)
- Towards shared goals (purpose)

If you don't currently work in a team, don't worry as you can do the exercises based on previous teams you have been in or you can use a team outside work, such as a sporting team, a band or drama group. The point is you will have to work in teams or across teams in the future as collaboration is and will continue to be a sought-after skill. I don't think I have ever had a job interview where they haven't asked me about how I work within a team. It's essential for most jobs.

If you manage a team or want to improve collaboration in your team, on our website there are lots of extra resources, games and exercises you can download to help you. You can find them at www. humanworksacademy.co.uk

Week four, day one

On day one you will learn:

- who you should spend time with
- what makes a successful team or team leader
- what sort of team player or team leader you are.

Exercise: Week four, day one
Leading a team

- -

 The people we spend time with can have a huge effect on our motivation, attitude and mindset. They can inspire and galvanise us, or equally, they can bring us down and suck our energy. As this week is all about collaboration and teamwork, it makes sense to focus our reset on the people you have in your life and if you want to make any changes.

List four to six people who you spend most time with outside your immediate family. Give each of them a mark out of 10 for the points below.

Helpfulness:

- Important in your career or business
- Knowledge and skills you can learn from or use
- Have a good network they can introduce you to

Total up the scores for each of them.

Attitudes and attributes

- Always positive, uplifting, giving energy, not sucking it
- Generous, caring, loyal, listener, empathetic
- Fun, cool, entertaining, charming

Again, total up the scores for each of them.

Now you have scores on helpfulness and attitudes and attributes, plot them in the table below. A low score will be less than 15.

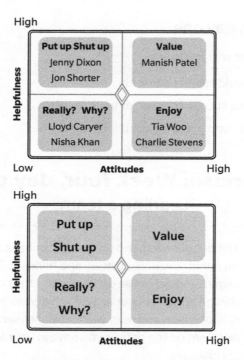

People you spend time with

- **High helpfulness/low attitude – Put up, shut up:** It's easy to moan about these types of people because they can be difficult to be around, but they are useful to you. So why waste time moaning? Instead, think about ways you can be more grateful and improve the relationship.

- **Low helpfulness/high attitude – Enjoy!:** Don't feel guilty about spending time with these people as they make you feel good. So see them often and give them 100% of your attention when you are with them as they deserve it.

- **High helpfulness/high attitude – Value:** If you have one or more of these in your six you are really lucky. So value them and say thank you as you can't afford to lose them.

- **Low helpfulness/low attitude – Really? Why?:** Do I need to say anything?

What does this tell you? Are you spending your time with the right people? What changes will you make?

 Research three successful teams from any walk of life or from any time in history. If you are a leader of a team look at the team leader's role in the success as well. To get you started, here are some ideas:

- The All Blacks, the New Zealand national rugby union team
- The Red Arrows
- NASA's Apollo 11

What made your chosen teams successful? What core skills, behaviours or values were essential for this team? What contribution does the team leader make?

What three key things have you learnt about successful teams?

 Ask for advice. Who do you know who works in a highly effective team or leads one? Connect with them in any way you like: face to face, phone or email. Ask them for advice on how you can be a more effective team member and what they think is the secret of their team's success. To get you started you could ask:

- Why do you think your team is successful?
- What qualities do you look for in an effective team member?
- What advice would you give me so I can collaborate more effectively?

 Today's stretch is to get feedback from your team (work or leisure) on your contribution and your ability to collaborate. Prepare a questionnaire to give you the feedback you want and give or send it out telling them why you want it and how much you would appreciate it.

If you're a team leader, you can ask for feedback on your leadership and encourage your team to feed back on the team as a whole and how it could improve.

Here are some possible questions to ask:

- What do you most value about my contribution to the team?
- How could I develop further to offer more value as a team member?
- How could I help and collaborate with you personally more?

Top tip

If you are not currently in a team at work or in your personal life, think back to when you were in one. What did you do well? What would you do differently next time you work in a team?

Based on today's exercises, write in your journal one thing you will start doing, one thing you will stop doing and one thing you will continue to do.

- -

Week four, day two

On day two you will learn:

- if you are an organiser or an adaptive
- how to collaborate more effectively with different types
- how to develop your team relationships.

Exercise: Week four, day two
What type of team member are you?

- -

One of the key things that can get in the way of effective teamwork and collaboration is a misunderstanding of the way we like to work.

Answer the following questions to discover whether you prefer to work in a structured and planned way or instead go with the flow and deal with things as they happen.

For each question, tick one of the two statements you identify most with.

1.	**(a)** I prefer to finish all my work before I relax or have fun **(b)** I am happy to stop work for fun as I can normally work late if need be	
2.	**(a)** I plan work to avoid rushing just before a deadline **(b)** I am stimulated by an approaching deadline	
3.	**(a)** I may appear a little inflexible as I like things planned and decided **(b)** I may appear to be loose and casual as I like to keep plans to a minimum	
4.	**(a)** I work consistently through the day **(b)** I work in bursts of energy throughout the day	

Mostly a) Organised: You will think sequentially and you value order and organisation. Your life is more scheduled and structured and you probably seek closure. You enjoy completing tasks and take deadlines seriously.

Key characteristics: Decisive, controlled, good at finishing, organised, structured, scheduled, responsible, likes closure, makes plans.

Mostly b) Adaptive: You will be adaptable and flexible, a random thinker who prefers to keep your options open. You will thrive on the unexpected and are open to change. You will probably be spontaneous and often juggle several projects at once.

Key characteristics: Adaptable, relaxed, less organised, carefree, spontaneous, changes track midway, keeps options open, dislikes routine.

Neither one of these types is better than the other. They are just different and you can see how collaborating with someone who works in a very dissimilar way could be frustrating and demotivating.

 In the warm-up you have identified if you are an adaptive or an organised type. In your journal work through the following:

- Who are you working with or have worked with who is the opposite type to you?

- What worked or is working with such a colleague (or colleagues)?

- What can you do now or in the future to improve your collaboration with this person (or people)?

The table below will help get you started.

Adapters	Organisers
Trust them and they will deliver	Keep them informed on how things are going, even if there is nothing to report
Be open to change and listen as they often have brilliant ideas	Use them to organise the time-bound elements
Appreciate them as they are great up against a deadline	Appreciate them as they are great at getting things finished

Based on day one and the first part of day two, what initiative could you take now or in the future to improve the way your team collaborate with each other.

At the next meeting you could suggest everyone takes the quiz on adapting and organising. Or you could do a more in-depth Myers Briggs report to help you all understand individual working needs and how you can collaborate more effectively.

Top tip

If you lead a team, visit our website for exercises you can do in team meetings on respect and appreciation of differences: www.humanworksacademy.co.uk

One great way to improve relationships, break down barriers and understand team members more effectively is to meet socially. Organise a team social, lunch, breakfast or go out for a drink. It's also a great opportunity to build on the skills of Engage, Listen and Empathise.

Virtual option, if you have a remote team, organize a team Zoom event, it could be a music quiz, happy hour, or team building event.

In your journal answer the following questions:

- What did you like most about today's activities, and why?
- What surprised you today and why?
- What did you learn from today's activities?

Week four, day three

On day three you will learn:

- different ways people negotiate a conflict
- your most likely style
- ideas on how to handle conflict in the future.

Exercise: Week four, day three
Handling conflict

Healthy teams will have disagreements. How you deal with these situations will either strengthen the team and build trust – or damage them and create doubts and negativity. This is especially important in the future as the old model of encouraging stable high-performing teams is rapidly changing. Teams need to form and storm constantly, meaning healthy conflict will be critical.

Think back to a time when you were in a conflict situation with someone:

- How did you approach it?
- What behaviours helped or hindered in resolving it?
- If you could turn back time how would you have preferred to tackle it?

All of the communication skills we have looked at so far will be extremely useful when dealing with challenge and conflict, and also will help you negotiate

153

the more difficult situations within your team and across teams. You are now going to look at a model that you can add to your toolkit.

Take this short quiz (the full version is on our website: http://humanworksacademy.co.uk).

Score yourself on each statement on a scale of 0 to 5: 0 = never, 1 = rarely, 2 = sometimes, 3 = occasionally, 4 = frequently and 5 = always.

1 If the other party's position seems very important to them, I may sacrifice my own position. ( ) C

2 I address problems and concerns directly without blame or judgment. ( ) E

3 I try to succeed by convincing the other party of the logic and benefits of my position. ( ) B

4 I try to find a compromise solution. ( ) D

5 I try to postpone discussions until I have had some time to think. ( ) A

6 Confronting someone about a problem is very uncomfortable for me. ( ) C

7 I remain calm and confident when faced with aggression or criticism. ( ) E

8 I see achievement as more important than relational issues. ( ) B

9 I try to find a fair combination of gains and losses for both of us. ( ) D

10 I find conflict stressful and will avoid it any way I can. ( ) A

Add up your scores as follows:

Scores for questions 1 and 6 ( ) = **Accommodation**

Scores for questions 2 and 7 ( ) = **Collaboration**

Scores for questions 3 and 8 ( ) = **Aggression**

Scores for questions 4 and 9 ( ) = **Compromise**

Scores for questions 5 and 10 ( ) = **Avoidance**

- **Avoidance:** You are eager to avoid confrontation, ignore problems, your own needs, and possibly the needs of others. This approach results at best in a delay or at worst in a lose/lose result where both relationships and results are sacrificed.

- **Competitive:** You focus exclusively on your own objectives, are eager to win, even at the expense of others. Trust and long-term results may be jeopardised in pursuit of this I win/you lose outcome.

- **Accommodation:** You focus too heavily on the relational dynamics and avoid attending to your own needs and interests. The risk is a you win/I lose outcome in which the other party gains at your expense.

- **Compromise:** You search for middle ground in resolving differences rather than pursuing potential solutions that often are found in common interests. It results in getting some of what you want and some of what you don't want. Compromise is our usual default but is less than a win/win since it results in a both kind of win/both kind of lose outcome.

- **Collaboration:** You stand up for your own interests, needs and values while honouring the interests, needs and values of others. You are able to balance results and relationships. Collaboration is always the best approach but it takes a greater investment of time and energy. In most cases, you'll find the results worth the effort.

What were your highest two scores?

What can you do to improve your skills when negotiating conflict? To get you started:

- Be more prepared.
- Work towards a shared objective.
- Ask questions, listen and be prepared to be creative with solutions.
- Focus on the interests of both parties and separate these from the emotions.

 Go to our website (http://humanworksacademy. co.uk) and download the full printable version of the conflict questionnaire. Give them out to your team-mates and at the next team meeting or gathering share the results.

Hold a discussion on how the team could deal with challenges and conflict more effectively.

Are you in any sort of conflict with anyone currently or trying to negotiate through a challenge? This can be at work or in your personal life.

Stage one

• What is the shared objective?

• What do you want out of the situation?

• What do they want out of the situation?

• What three things could you do to move you both closer to the shared objective?

Stage two

Arrange to meet or talk (this could be over Skype, WhatsApp or Zoom) and take the first step towards solving the issue.

Top tip

If you don't have any conflict right now (lucky you!) go back to the warm-up exercise and the issue you looked at then and imagine you could go back in time. How would you deal with this differently?

In your journal answer the following questions:

• What were the key things you learnt about managing conflict today?

• How can you use this to improve your teamwork and collaboration?

Week four, day four

On day four you will learn:

• why passive aggressive behaviour is destructive

• the difference between feeding back and feeding forward

• how to feed forward.

Exercise: Week four, day four
Feeding forward

- -

 Passive aggressive behaviour is the most toxic and destructive behaviour in the workplace. Here is an example:

'I'm so fed up with Manish leaving everything to the last minute. It means I don't know where I am and it stresses me out.'

'My manager is not giving me any opportunity to develop my presentation skills. It's not fair.'

Both of these examples of talking behind someone's back are likely to damage trust. They are unhelpful because there is no opportunity to change things. Without the open dialogue there is so much room for assumptions, misunderstandings and getting things plain wrong.

To collaborate effectively, you need to create a safe and open environment where everyone can give each other feedback that is helpful and supportive. As hierarchy is more and more stripped back, feedback is not just a team leader's responsibility – it's everyone's.

Answer these questions in your journal:

- How do you feel about giving feedback to others?
- How do you feel about giving upward feedback (to your manager)?
- What holds you back from giving feedback?

 Having a growth mindset means seeing feedback as an opportunity to learn, but giving feedback is sometimes more difficult than receiving it. In the answers to the questions in the warm-up, did you say that you are worried about hurting people's feelings or you don't want to rock the boat and make things uncomfortable? The chances are you don't know how to give feedback in a way that's helpful. I do a lot of management and leadership training and it's the thing most team leaders want help with.

What is your intention? If you are frustrated, angry or disappointed and you're giving feedback to get back at someone, it will come across loud and clear. If you squeeze an orange, what do you get? Juice! Humans are the same: squeeze us and the true intent comes out. Deal with these emotions first or express them openly. Otherwise, you will create the bad feeling you were hoping to avoid.

Let's say you want to give feedback to Manish who is more of an adaptive type and you are an organiser. On projects together, he leaves everything to the last minute, he works like crazy just before the deadline and it leaves you exhausted and stressed. Imagine you give him this feedback: 'Manish you are always so disorganised and last minute, and it's stressing me out.'

What is wrong with this? First of all, it's judgmental (always so disorganised) and second, it's about what happened rather than what you want to happen.

Instead you can feed forward: 'Manish we work quite differently and it would really help me if you could let me know how you're doing on a project so I don't stress out. I can then leave you to get on with it.'

This is formative, helpful and supportive and has no judgments. This sort of feedback changes the culture of a working relationship and makes collaboration easier and more successful.

In your journal turn the following feedback into feed forward:

Feedback: 'You always have too many slides in your presentation with too much information on each slide and I saw some of the audience zone out last time you presented.'

Feedback: 'When we go to meetings together you never contribute and leave it all up to me.'

 Decide on some feedback you need to deliver to someone in your workplace. It can be someone in your team or another team or your boss. Focus on one specific area for improvement. Write in your journal how you will say it in a feed forward manner, read it out and keep refining it until it sounds right.

If you lead a team check out the website for team exercises on giving and receiving feedback: http://humanworksacademy.co.uk

Top tip

Read out your feedback to someone else outside your work and ask them how they would feel if they got this feedback.

Now go and give your feedback. It's definitely preferable to do this face to face, but if you work remotely you could do this on a video call, or worst-case scenario by email. Be careful as email can be misunderstood and it's there forever so get someone to look at it first.

In your journal answer the following questions:

- How do you now feel about feeding forward?
- How will this make a difference to the way you collaborate with others in the future?
- What do you still need to work on?

Week four, day five

On day five you will learn:

- how to start with Why?
- great ideas for team meetings and away days
- the Critical Success Factor model.

Exercise: Week four, day five
Start with why

In 26 years of training I have come across some great ideas that are really useful to help teams and individuals collaborate more successfully. I am sharing a few of my favourites today but there are loads more on the website: http://humanworksacademy.co.uk

Stage one

Watch Simon Sinek's TED talk: How great leaders inspire action.

This TED talk is brilliantly simple. If you want real collaboration you need to know your purpose and vision for your group or team. which needs to be clear and visible to everyone.

People don't buy what you do; they buy why you do it.

Simon Sinek

Stage two

Here are some 'Why' statements to inspire you:

- Transportation as reliable as running water, everywhere for everyone. (Uber)
- Make a contribution to the world by making tools for the mind that advance humankind. (APPLE)
- To improve everyday life for all.

Stage three

Whether you are working on your own, in a small project team, running your own business or you are a CEO of a large company, you need a purpose, a why. Start the process now and work through the questions below for whatever you are working on:

- Why do you get out of bed in the morning?
- Why does your job or team exist?
- Why should that matter to anyone else?

Top tip

Keep playing around with your purpose statement until it feels right, then leave it a while and come back to it. Does it still feel right? Then shout it to the rooftops!

For team leaders this makes a great away day activity.

You are going to see how collaborative meetings can work with Edward de Bono's 'Thinking hats'.

This way of running a meeting has saved my marriage – and that's no exaggeration. I work with my husband and my son and we are extroverts with very strong opinions. This system allows us to keep focused and stay friends. It is a valuable tool for group discussions so you can work through ideas and make decisions.

The hats are a way to control the thinking and discussion. By the way, these are metaphorical hats but it could be fun to have real ones.

Blue hat	One person wears this hat as the facilitator, controlling the hats that are used and when
White hat	Data, facts, what is known or you need to know
Red hat	Feelings, hunches, instinct and intuition
Black hat	Devil's advocate, negatives, potential problems, what won't work
Yellow hat	Value and benefits, what will work
Green hat	Ideas, brainstorming, creative solutions, alternatives, new ideas (no judgment or critique of ideas)

There is no set way to run a meeting, but I find it's useful to jointly agree who is wearing the blue hat and the order of the hats. The facilitator then makes sure the thinking method is stuck to, but the team has decided the order.

Critical success factors is a great model to set a strategic plan.

• **Step 1:** Establish your project's why and strategic goals (see warm-up).

• **Step 2:** For each strategic goal, ask yourself 'What area of business or project activity is essential to achieve this goal?' Evaluate the list of activities to find the absolute essential elements for achieving success. These are your Critical Success Factors (CSF).

• **Step 3:** Identify how you can achieve each CSF. These are your actions.

- **Step 4:** Communicate these insights to the team and the business.
- **Step 5:** Keep monitoring and re-evaluating your CSFs to ensure you keep progressing towards your project's or team's aims.

 Why not bring this whole week together by taking the initiative and organising an away day for your team or group to create a team charter; this can also be done remotely, if you all work from home or in different countries. You could even run it using the thinking hats. This would consist of:

- the why for the project
- strategic goals for the project
- critical success factors to deliver on the goals
- desirable behaviours for the team

Top tip

I have run a number of away days for large companies over the years and if you go to our website (www.humanworksacademy. co.uk) you can find examples of some of these team charters and how to run your own team charter away day.

 • undesirable behaviours to avoid for the team.

It's the end of the week, and it's time for a walk to take some time to think through your week on a reflection ramble. To get you started:

- What was the best thing that happened all week?
- Where did you add value or help someone?
- What have been your 'aha' moments and how will they change what you do in the future?

Progress check

This is the penultimate week which had lots of great tools for you to try out now and in the future. It's now time to reflect on your week and make a final goal for the Inspire week.

Weekly reflection

Answer the following questions in your journal honestly and openly:

- Did I do something that was out my comfort zone? How did it make me feel?
- What did I learn that would help me achieve my goals?
- How am I changing and what examples have I got that prove this?
- What can I do better or differently next week?
- What was the best thing that happened to me this week?
- What did I discover new about myself?
- What will I keep working on to improve myself?

Human roadmap

Go back to your human roadmap and review it carefully:

- Do you want to change anything?
- Have you stayed true to your personal values?
- Are you using your strengths?
- Are you developing the key areas you identified need working on, and what progress are you making?

SMARTER goals

You set a SMARTER goal at the end of last week. Now review how you did by answering the following questions in your journal:

- Was this goal easier or harder than expected?
- Overall, are you happy with your progress? If you are, then great! If not, work out why and fix the problem.
- What are you doing well towards this goal? And keep doing it!
- What do you need to do better to achieve this goal? And do it better!
- Are you enjoying this goal, or at least excited about the end result? Reward yourself for achieving mini-goals and milestones to keep you on your journey. Remember, the end result needs to be something you really want.

Top tip

Remember the five skills overlap, so each week you should be working on them all. This will make you more than ready for Inspire as it incorporates all of the previous skills.

In your journal set another SMARTER goal for next week. It can be something related to the previous weeks that you want to carry on working on, or it can be related to Week five Inspire. We will review this goal in next week's progress check.

chapter 9

Week five: Inspire

Storytelling, influencing and motivating people with your ideas

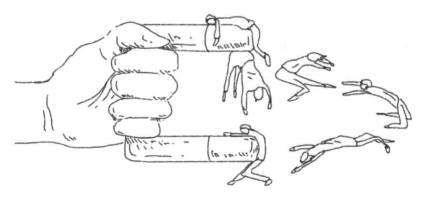

It's always been important to be able to inspire and influence others as we are all salespeople, selling something. A product or a service are the obvious ones, but what about selling your vision, ideas, solutions, or even yourself. You don't have to be famous or in the news to inspire. Sometimes the most inspiring people in the world are completely unknown, because they are doing their thing locally for something they believe in, or they are inspiring their team on a project they all care about. Think about Captain Tom Moore the war veteran, who raised the money by **walking** laps in his garden, **during lockdown**.

You might think of influencing and inspiring as something you do at work, but what is more important than inspiring the people most important to you such as your partner, parents or children.

Inspire means to excite, encourage or breathe life into. Imagine the world without inspiration and inspiring people. It's almost like a world without breath and life. Think about this for just one minute: there would be no music, no art, no films or TV, no beautiful buildings, no fashion, no technology and no books. It would be a very dull place. It would also be a very selfish and miserable place, because inspiration is about having a vision and a cause, moving people to make a difference.

This week will be exciting and inspiring but it's also a tough one. By the end of this week, you will you have improved your ability to motivate, influence and tell your story. If you can successfully inspire others, it can impact so many areas in your life, from getting the kids to empty the dishwasher to feeling happy and fulfilled.

Week five, day one

On day one you will learn:

- how to reframe self-limiting beliefs
- what you can learn from inspiring people
- how to inspire others to a cause.

Exercise: Week five, day one
Positive self-belief

- -

Positive people with belief and conviction inspire people, so the reset this week is even more important. What story are you telling yourself because what we tell ourselves can be a self-fulfilling prophecy?

Rate yourself 1 to 5 on the scale for each self-limited belief, 1 being no way and 5 being yes that's me.

Self-limiting belief	Explanation and examples	Rating
All-or-nothing thinking	Absolutes and extreme terms 'I always make the same mistakes'	1 2 3 4 5
Magnification or 'awfulising'	Blowing things out of proportion, making mountains out of molehills 'If we don't hit deadline, we are all out of a job'	1 2 3 4 5
Minimisation	Making excuses for our successes or strengths 'I was lucky. Getting the contract was nothing really'	1 2 3 4 5
Personalisation	Blaming ourselves unfairly 'We didn't get that contract and I am totally to blame'	1 2 3 4 5
Phoney-ism	Fearing others may find out we are not the person we say we are 'My presentations have been great so far but one day I'll make a mistake and they will discover how useless I really am'	1 2 3 4 5
Fortune-telling	Predicting the worse-case scenario, often by using insufficient evidence 'I've got off to a bad start today. That means the rest of the day will be a write-off'	1 2 3 4 5

For any you scored 3 or less on, ask yourself why you think you have these beliefs. The reasons could be various, but usually it's because of a bad experience or societal programming.

Next accept that these beliefs are simply not true and then reframe them into something you can work with.

Here are two examples of mine:

- **Minimisation:** I have this belief because I was told it was rude and arrogant to boast. So reframed this is: I worked really hard to get that contract and my presentation was really well rehearsed. I deserved to get it.

- **Phoney-ism:** I was told at school that I was always winging it. So reframred this is: I have years of experience and I have made mistakes but I am now really good at what I do.

 This is one of those exercises that might make you raise an eyebrow, but trust me if you go for it it's very powerful.

Choose three famous people you are inspired by. They can be dead or alive but they need to be from different walks of life. Mine would be Mother Teresa, Steve Jobs and John Lennon.

Why do your three people inspire you? Now imagine you are having a drink with them and they have all the time in the world for you. In your mind ask each of them the following questions and write down the answers that pop into your head:

- Why do you think you are/were able to inspire so many people?

- What bit of advice would you give me if I wanted to inspire others to a cause?

- How did you deal with doubters and cynics?

 Hopefully you got some surprising and useful insights from this exercise.

Bringing you back to reality, now think of people in your real life that inspire you. To get you started it might be one of the following:

- your boss
- a parent or grandparent

- a teacher or coach
- a colleague
- a friend.

Through whatever medium you feel most comfortable with (face to face, phone, video conferencing, email), tell them they are an inspiration and why. And then ask them to answer the same three questions from the warm-up.

I am really excited to get you started on this week's stretch because it is going to run right across the whole week and it inspires me just thinking about it.

Choose a cause or charity you feel strongly about that realistically you could help in some way, either by volunteering or raising money. By the end of the week you will need to inspire other people to do this with you, so bear that in mind when you make your choice.

Top tip

Start recording your journey this week, with photos, videos, anything about your cause. Share them on our special Facebook group for the book: www.facebook.com/groups/thehumanworksacademy. The best three will be invited to be part of a special podcast.

Based on the work you have done today – getting advice from inspiring people –reflect on the following:

- What did they have in common?
- What were the key themes that came out?
- What have you learnt that inspires you?

Week five, day two

On day two you will learn:

- what type of influencer you are
- how to inspire and influence different personality types
- how to develop a successful network.

Exercise: Week five, day two
The art of influencing people

In previous chapters we looked at introvert and extrovert, thinker and feeler types. Combining these two together can give us an insight into how the different types are inspired and motivated.

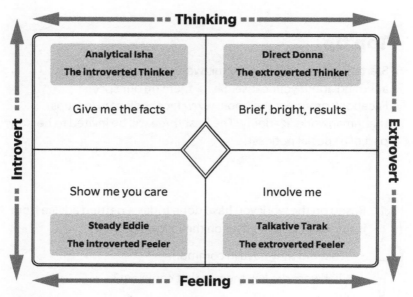

Personality quadrant

Each type needs a different influencing strategy, but it all rests on you telling the right story to prove your point. A story about someone else's success is 17% more likely to move people to action than facts and data, but it needs to match their individual preferences. If you are giving a presentation to more than one person you will need to include something for each type.

Types	Positive behaviours	Influencing strategy
Analytical Aisha (IT) Always wants more information. Difficult to read and engage in an open conversation because she's not likely to share her emotions.	Be prepared – know your details and facts Send proposals in advance Quiet conviction	'It's worked before' Paint the picture, how you overcame challenges, got things right Include the detail that proves your point
Steady Eddie (IF) Soft-spoken, gentle, warm, focused on others, not personal results. Quiet, difficult to read. Wants to make sure it works for all. Indecisive	Don't be pushy Listen and understand Reassure	'I'm here to help' Tell stories of how you considered the people and involved them in the success, and how they benefited
Direct Donna (ET) Direct and forceful, wants to control the decisions. Challenges ideas to be sure they deliver results. Doesn't want detail. Needs a results-focused and goal-oriented presentation	Be assertive Have a strong conviction Keep things brief Focus on results	**'Don't miss out'** Tell stories about outstanding results and how you were an agent for change Give them the proof with real quotes from stakeholders
Talkative Tarak (EF) Outgoing, wants to connect. Easily distracted, goes off track to share thoughts and stories. Prefers enthusiastic, emotional arguments, bored by details.	Be passionate and enthusiastic Connect with them socially Be open, friendly and authentic	'You will make a difference' Tell them a story with passion and emotions. Move them to believe they can also change the world.

You are now going to build a network of who to influence. Add this exercise to your toolkit, use it regularly to inspire and influence the key people who matter in your life in the right way. This is a work version.

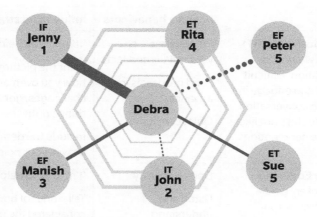

Network analysis

- Draw out a network diagram like the example above.
- Write your name in a circle in the middle.
- Around the outside of the diagram write in all the people inside or outside your department or company who have an impact on the success of your career. This is your network.
- Draw lines from these colleagues into the circle containing your name representing the health of the relationship (based on your rapport, communication and your deliverables or service to them). Use the following key to evaluate these:

  - .... Fragile
  - --------- Vulnerable
  - _____ Steady
  - _____ Healthy

- Add what influencer type they are: IT, ET, IF, EF.
- Give them a number representing one of the following:

1 Advocate

2 Supporter

3 Blocker

4 Critic

5 Influencer

Now you have clarity on your network, pick two you want to work on who are important to your career right now.

Top tip

It doesn't have to be someone you have a fragile or vulnerable relationship with. You could choose a healthy advocate or a steady supporter to help you.

 For your two priorities you chose in the core exercise, work through the following:

- Why do you want to influence and inspire them?
- What story will you tell?
- What are the 'blockages' to being more influential with these people?

Have one key action for each.

Take one small step towards each of the actions you have decided on today, no matter how small, and keep working at it.

 Now you have chosen your cause and are feeling inspired and passionate about it, think about ways you could help and move others to get involved. Ask friends and colleagues for ideas, do some brainstorming with them as you never know they might be inspired too. To get you started think along these lines:

- Use your skills (marketing, building, selling).
- Raise money.

- Promote your cause.
- Do the work (pick up litter, build a playground, paint a village hall).

Reflect on how you like to be influenced. Be aware this week of people influencing or selling to you.

Week five, day three

On day three you will learn:

- ethical selling and influencing skills
- push and pull behaviours
- how to use push and pull to sell something.

Exercise: Week five, day three
Selling and influencing

Influence and persuasion are two of the most powerful traits that can help you achieve your desired level of success.

Ian Berry, author of *Influence: The Science Behind Persuasion*

Selling: To persuade someone of the merits of something.
Influencing: To affect or change how someone or something develops, behaves, or thinks.

Selling and influencing are often seen as dirty words, because we associate selling with pushy car salespeople and influencing with power-hungry politicians. I run sales and influencing courses and work with architects selling their ideas for amazing social housing projects, charities looking for funding and consultants trying to influence a change in the education system.

It's not the selling or influencing that's the problem – it's the people who give them a bad name.

Write in your journal about a time when you were on the receiving end of poor selling or influencing. What were the behaviours? What effect did it have on you and why? To get you started, these words may help:

- pushy and aggressive
- didn't listen
- on their agenda
- dishonest.

 The three Ps is a way to influence and persuade which is ethical and natural:

- Pull – ask, listen, understand – establishes opportunity
- Push – tell, advocate, articulate – demonstrates conviction
- Potential value – delivers real value to them

Pull behaviours	Push behaviours	Potential value
Open and follow up questions to establish needs or potential interest in your proposal	Clear, concise, persuasive arguments, delivered with confidence and conviction	Made relevant by linking them to the stakeholders' needs
Inviting challenge and asking for feedback	Overcoming objections and resistance with evidence and proof	Linking answers back to how it will help and benefit them
Open to negotiation and compromise	Standing firm on areas you feel strongly about	Re affirming the benefits

Here is an example of the three Ps being used in a positive way in an interview.

Interviewer: Tell me how you can add value to our business?

Interviewee: (Pull) I feel I have a lot to offer. May I ask what you are specifically looking for in the ideal candidate?

Interviewer: The most important thing for us is they are a team player, able to communicate effectively and maintain successful relationships under pressure.

Interviewee: (Push) In my current role we are responsible for developing new products and hit deadlines under extreme pressure. I maintain successful relationships by taking the time to ask my colleagues how they are doing and if they need help. I am also happy to ask for help if I need it as I think this open communication develops trust. (Potential value)

The interviewee was able to give a more tailored answer to the original question, thereby addressing the interviewer's needs directly rather than taking a stab in the dark and going for a 'Let's throw a load of mud at the wall and hope it sticks' technique.

It's your turn. Think of a book you have read recently that you loved (it could be this one!). In your journal think of questions you could ask to establish the value of your chosen book, and all the great things about the book. And finally what the potential value is to your 'customer'. I have given you one example to get you started.

Pull (questions you could ask)	Push (facts and advantages)	Potential value
1. What type of books do you like?	1. This book is easy to read with lots of ideas	1. You are more likely to get the results you want
2.	2.	2.
3.	3.	3.
4.	4.	4.
5.	5.	5.

 Using the work you have done in the core exercise, your challenge is to sell your chosen book to as many people as you can today using the three Ps.

Top tip

When you put forward any idea or suggestion in your head ask 'So what?'; this will help you to talk about the value to the other person.

The three Ps is a great model for preparing to sell an idea. Repeat the process for your cause or charity, and this time do it in more depth, building your understanding of the potential value of your idea. You will be using this at the end of the week.

In your journal answer the following questions:

- What did you like most about today's activities, and why?
- What surprised you today and why?
- What did you learn from today's activities?

Week five, day four

On day four you will learn:

- why stories are powerful
- how to structure a story
- how to create a personal story that sells you and your cause.

Exercise: Week five, day four
The power of storytelling

Today is about inspiring through storytelling. Think back to a time when you were inspired to act after hearing a story. Recently the 4ocean project story moved me to join the whole of my family to the movement. A well-crafted story is often more powerful than any other means of persuasion.

There is a lot of scientific evidence to prove we are wired to be moved and inspired by stories, and what better way to learn about this than from a TED talk on storytelling: The magical science of storytelling by David JP Phillips.

Watch it on the train, in the gym or during your coffee break. It's fantastic.

 Choose a fictional story you love and work through my example below making notes in your journal on how your story delivers on each part.

- **Scene-setting:** *The Hobbit* is one of my all-time favourite stories and the opening pages are beautifully descriptive and detailed, bringing to life the Shires and Bilbo's hobbit hole. Early on we care about the characters.

- **A watershed moment:** A moment of truth, a tragedy or challenge the characters have to face. In *The Hobbit* it's Gandalf arriving at Bilbo Baggins' house to invite him on a terrifying quest.

- **The journey:** A conflict, struggle or a journey our hero finds themselves on. It might be an emotional journey rather than a real one and it is fraught with challenges and discoveries, leading to learning and growth.

- **The climax:** A dramatic event, the end of the journey or the big fight. In *The Hobbit* it's the fight against the dragon.

- **The fall out:** The immediate events after the big climax. How do the characters fare and how are they dealing with the consequences?

- **The resolution:** How did it end up and what happened to the characters? What have they learnt? What can we learn from it? Maybe it has a deep and powerful final message.

 Go back to your roadmap to humanness and taking the elevator pitch you were asked to write, use the structure above and turn it into a story.

My example

Twenty-one years ago, I was standing outside a recruitment agency hoping to change my life. It was a winter's night, dank, dark and chilly and I felt all my doubts and fears cheeping in. I was a mum to three young children who depended on me, so how could I take such a big risk? I stepped into an old red, smelly phone box and rang my husband in tears. I told him I couldn't do it, 'I'm not a trainer, I'm kidding myself.' Gently and calmly he told me it was ok and to come home and we would work it out.

I stepped out of the phone box and into the building. The interview went unbelievably well and I was given my first free-lance training work. In that moment when I nearly gave up and went home, I felt a calling, a purpose. It was my chance to make a difference to people's lives and do something I loved.

Since then I have worked with some amazing companies and been privileged to help individuals reach their potential. In 21 years not once have I regretted that moment and never given up on a dream. Push yourselves past that fear zone and who knows where it will take you.

Compare this to my elevator pitch in Chapter 4.

Top tip

This is work in progress, so it takes time to get this right. It is something you should keep working on. You might have different versions of your story for different people and situations.

 Why did you choose the cause you are working on this week? Was it because of a story? Do some research on great current causes, watch their videos, listen to the stories, and jot down in your journal anything you like.

Start to map out your story to sell your cause. This is a really inspiring way to spend an evening so why not involve your family or friends.

What were the key things you learnt about storytelling today? How can you use storytelling in your work?

- -

Week five, day five

On day five you will learn how to:

- develop a core message
- improve your delivery
- present your ideas.

Exercise: Week five, day five
Inspire others!

- -

Today we are going to get you ready to inspire others to work with you on your cause. Because you are actually doing and living this you won't forget and you can come back to this process at any time you need to inspire others.

Using all the work you have done this week on your cause, before you do anything else you need to answer some important questions in your journal about your audience:

- Who are you trying to inspire?
- What's important to them?
- What three questions would they want answered?
- What do you want them to think, feel and do?
- Why will they listen to you?

Top tip

The secret to great presenting is to talk to your audience about them rather than at them about you.

 Your core message is really important for any type of presentation, whether it's to 500 people or just one important one. A core message is the main theme that should run through the presentation. It means you can then choose the right story to tell, the most appropriate facts to include and the most relevant visuals to use (if any).

To help you understand what I mean, Elon Musk is probably one of the most visionary men of our time. The core message for his company Tesla is simple and sums up what they want the world to know about them: To accelerate the world's transition to sustainable energy.

I mentioned my commitment to the 4ocean charity, and its core message is:

 One Ocean – One Mission: Let's end the Ocean plastic crisis together.

Have a go yourself – come up with the core message for your cause.

Now bring everything together and create your presentation. Use the points below to map it out:

- **Profile your audience:** Notes on your audience from the warm-up questions.

- **My core message:** Write this in one sentence.

- **My story:** Make sure it links to the core message.

- **The Value – the three Ps:** Don't forget to sell the value.

- **How you can make it memorable:** Key facts, quotes, images, etc.

- **A strong call to action:** Remind them of the value and what you or they want to happen next.

In a quiet room, record yourself. I know what you're thinking, but rehearsing and watching yourself is the best way to improve. If you are really brave you can ask someone to give you feedback. Steven Jobs said for any 30 minute presentation, he would do 30 hours of research, 30 hours of planning and putting it all together and 30 hours of rehearsal.

Are you ready? Now go and change the world!

It's the end of the week, and it's time for a walk – your reflection ramble – to think through your week. To get you started consider:

- What was the best thing that happened all week?

- Where did you add value or help someone?

- What have been your 'aha' moments and how will they change what you do in the future?

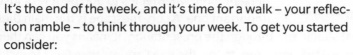

Progress check

Congratulations, you've done it! What a fantastic week to end on. I can't help but smile to myself as all of you are out there inspiring others to follow a cause. You've come a long way but don't give up now – one more progress check.

Weekly reflection

Answer the following questions in your journal honestly and openly:

- Did I do something that was out my comfort zone? How did it make me feel?

- What did I learn that would help me achieve my goals?

- How am I changing and what examples have I got that prove this?
- What can I do better or differently next week?
- What was the best thing that happened to me this week?
- What did I discover new about myself?
- What will I keep working on to improve myself?

Human roadmap

Go back to your human roadmap and review it carefully:

- Do you want to change anything?
- Have you stayed true to your personal values?
- Are you using your strengths?
- Are you developing the key areas you identified need working on, and what progress are you making?
- How are you feeling about your personal story now?

SMARTER goals

You set a SMARTER goal at the end of last week. Now review how you did by answering the following questions in your journal:

- Was this goal easier or harder than expected?
- Overall, are you happy with your progress? If you are, then great! If not, work out why and fix the problem.
- What are you doing well towards this goal? And keep doing it!
- What do you need to do better to achieve this goal? And do better!
- Are you enjoying this goal, or at least excited about the end result? Reward yourself for achieving mini-goals and milestones to keep you on your journey. Remember, the end result needs to be something you really want.

Top tip

Celebrate your success and go and buy a new journal. It's a great habit to keep and you can use it to continue your journey.

chapter 10

Keep following the roadmap

Congratulations! You have worked through five weeks of the masterclass (that's 130 exercises). You have mastered the ability to connect easily and naturally using SPARK. Your listening will be getting you noticed as people realise you are not just on your own agenda. You will also be much more self-aware and aware of others, making it easier to understand and appreciate the people you work with (and live with).

Empathy will be conscious and natural and you have a whole toolkit to help you and your team collaborate more effectively now and in the future. Your ability to inspire and influence can help motivate and move people when you need it and you will now be sensitive to how important a healthy mindset is.

But this is not the end and it's not the beginning either. That would be such a cliché! You have now developed new habits and are fitter than ever in your human skills as you will be thinking differently and acting differently. And hopefully you are inspired and motivated to keep learning and growing. All of this means you are already standing out as a better employee, colleague, partner, parent or friend and you are ahead of the curve for that future career you dreamed about.

The key thing is to not fall back (which is what this chapter is about), but to remain inspired to keep going and if possible inspire others to get on the journey with you. Every single one of us have people in our lives who could benefit from being on their phone less, connecting more and being open to other people's needs. You can't force people to go to the gym but if you offer to go with them, they are more likely to go.

I asked myself if I had a personal trainer for five weeks at the gym and I was now on my own, what would I want as a follow-up to keep me motivated and in shape. The following final exercises came to me.

Let's take stock

- What have been the highlights of the masterclass, the most enjoyable and memorable moments?
- How are you feeling now?
- Set a timer for 60 seconds and write down in your journal everything you have learnt from reading this book.
- What can you do now to go above and beyond in the future?

Send out your feedback email again

This will be so much easier this time I promise, draft it in any way you want but make sure you appreciate the person for their time, and tell them about your journey. Then ask them the following three questions:

- What positive improvements have you noticed about my human skills since the first email? Please give me specifics.
- How would you describe me to someone who didn't know me?
- What else could I do to improve my human skills?

Progress pie chart

Give yourself a mark out of 10 for each of the key skills and fill in the pie chart. This will give you a nice snapshot of where you are now in terms of the areas you are strongest in and where you need to do more work. Do this every few months, as it gives you the opportunity to keep on top of things.

Growth mindset ( )

Engage ( )

Listen ( )

Empathise ( )

Collaborate ( )

Inspire ( )

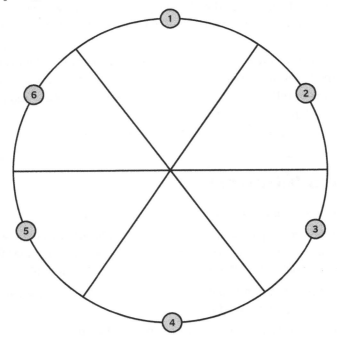

Progress pie chart

Top tip

If you look at this every couple of months, it will keep your awareness up and help you to check in with yourself. Are you still confident talking to people or are you starting to pick up bad habits? If you notice your pie chart dipping in any areas, go back to those weeks in the masterclass and redo the exercises to remind yourself of what you need to do to keep the skills fit and healthy.

Letter to a better self

This is a really surprisingly powerful exercise (the simple ones often are). Write a short letter to yourself in the future, laying out the work and personal goals you want to achieve in the next 12 months. This is a completely private and reflective personal exercise, so take your time and really describe where you want to be and what you want to be doing.

Doing this has worked for me and it can be uncanny when you open the letter in 12 months. So don't forget about it, set yourself a diary note to tell you where you put it and when to open it and put it somewhere it can't get lost.

Below are some ideas on what to put in our letter.

Dear future me

- Praise your future self on your success so far.
- Write down your work and personal goals and how you think you will need to achieve them. (Do you need to learn something new? Do you need to change jobs? Travel?)
- Write down three positive things that you do really well and appreciate yourself for them.
- Finally tell yourself to keep smiling and be human!

From past me

Ongoing training programme

This one is easy as you have this book and can go back to the masterclass whenever you need to. Also on the website www.humanworksacademy.co.uk are booster exercises on all the skills to keep you motivated and interested. I have also created some extra materials for specific job areas:

- Customer service and hospitality
- Sales and account management
- Management and leadership

There is also the opportunity to attend one of our live 'Human Works' weekends. These are run face to face and on Zoom.

You will find details of these on our website and Facebook group: www.facebook.com/groups/thehumanworksacademy/

Celebrate success

Recognising and celebrating success is a very powerful motivator because it reinforces the meaning behind all that hard work and it shows appreciation for your achievements. This boosts your self-esteem and motivates you to take the next step towards achieving your goals. Look back at your social media descriptions and sell yourself, tell your story, how you stand out; it's ok to big yourself up, you deserve it, and ask for recommendations.

Share your stories and inspire others. You are now invited to join our special Facebook group: www.facebook.com/groups/thehumanworksacademy/ so you can share your journey with others. I will be checking in to see how the storytelling skills are doing. I will also post regular booster exercises to keep you on your toes.

And finally, despite everything for the humans that stand out the future is bright.

The working environment is changing rapidly, and you will see more and more alarmist headlines about us being replaced by robots taking our jobs. It's true there are increasing amounts of automation: checkouts

at supermarkets and automatic check-in at airports. There is technology that could replace bar staff, waiting staff and coffee baristas. The large retail outlets in the high streets are closing because of online shopping and manufacturing companies are replacing people employed to do repetitive tasks. There are also more robots coming into healthcare, journalism, law and recruitment – and don't even get me started on where it will go in IT and technology.

But you are human and you are the customer. Is this what you want? Do you want your beer, glass of wine or breakfast served by a robot? Even during the Corona Virus most of us wanted the human touch.

In truth, we have a choice: if we want quick, easy, cheap, efficient and cold we will be able to get it, but if we want an experience, warmth and human interaction we can have it. But we will still want to pay quickly and not have to queue, so even in the more human businesses and services we will want to make the most of automation and technology. And why wouldn't we as it's brilliant?

The use of technology speeding up ordering and paying for food and drink is freeing up time for the human bar tender or waiter to smile, talk and even entertain us. The trains aren't far off driving themselves so the train guard is looking after our needs and interacting with the customers. In the very near future, the dangerous, repetitive, frankly soul-destroying jobs will be done by robots. Lawyers, doctors and nurses will be able to spend more time empathising and caring for people rather than doing data-driven diagnostics that robots do so much better.

The key thing is to take responsibility for your own learning. There will be countless opportunities for people with great human skills in lots of different types of businesses. While the future might be filled with artificial intelligence, deep learning and indescribable amounts of data, uniquely human skills will be the ones that matter. Machines can't write a symphony, design a building, teach a college course or lead a team. The robots won't be the competition because you won't be able to compete for the jobs they will be doing and wouldn't want to. The competition will be other humans. You have the choice – don't be a human robot and get left behind – stand out instead!

Don't stop there!

I am always here to help, so if you need any further support do contact me on debra@humanworksacademy.co.uk I promise to get back to you. If you have any feedback or thoughts about this book, I will be happy to hear them.

For further details of our Human Works weekends, visit our website at www. humanworksacademy.co.uk You can get full versions of the quizzes in this book and access to your own personalised reports, with lots of bonus materials to keep your human skills in tip-top condition. This is where you can get the full digital version of the Human Robot quiz.

As a reader of this book, you are invited to a very special private Facebook group at www.facebook.com/groups/thehumanworksacademy to share your journey, swap stories and get advice from others. I will regularly post my own thoughts, ideas and resources exclusively for you.

 And finally, if you're interested in corporate training workshops for your team, then visit www.dramatictrainingsolutions.co.uk

Index
